ESSENTIAL
MANNERS FOR
MEN

Also from the Emily Post Institute

ESSENTIAL
MANNERS FOR
MEN

• SECOND EDITION •

WHAT TO DO, WHEN TO DO IT, AND WHY

PETER POST

WILLIAM MORROW
An Imprint of HarperCollinsPublishers

FIRST EDITION

Based on the design of Ralph L. Fowler

Library of Congress Cataloging-in-Publication Data has been applied for.

ISBN 978-0-06-208041-7

24 25 26 27 28 LBC 19 18 17 16 15

For thirty-nine years we have lived together, shared children, owned a business together, gone shopping every week together, renovated one house and built another together. She introduced me to two of the passions of my life: Italy and yoga. We have worked together at The Emily Post Institute for the past ten years. She edits virtually everything I write. She knows and lives by what etiquette is as well as any person I know. Certainly she has corrected me more than a few times, and, as much as I hate to say it, she was almost always right.

Throughout this book she is referred to as "my wife."

But here, it is my pleasure to thank Tricia for all her help and patience working with me on my columns and blogs and in making this book possible.

CONTENTS

PART TWO: SOCIAL LIFE

PART THREE: ON THE JOB

MEN WANT ANSWERS

A lot of water has gone under the bridge since *Essential Manners for Men* was first published in October 2003. Then, *metrosexual* was the watch-word and *Queer Eye for the Straight Guy* was a runaway success as one of the newest reality television series. All of a sudden the focus was on men and their self-improvement—and men were finally waking up.

This isn't surprising to me. Since 2003 I've conducted seminars around the country for corporations, government entities, and universities. Without exception, every one of those seminars was filled with men who wanted to know what to do in their personal and professional lives to help them be as successful as possible.

These men engage me during the seminars, and they want to have their questions answered afterward as well. The questions always come back to one concept: "I want to look like I know what to do. I don't want to be embarrassed." Men crave that sense of confidence that comes from being sure of how to act—because once they're sure, they can turn their focus to the people they are with and to building the relationship. When they are hesitant and unsure, they look lost, and they know it.

For me, the best part of having written this book is the opportunity I've had to change people's lives. When the first edition was released, it was timed to be a great gift book—and it was. Parents repeatedly told me how they liked to observe which present caught their sons' attention on Christmas morning. They were amazed to find their sons off in a corner, reading the book, page after page.

One young man wrote me. It seems his life was going down the tubes.

His relationship with his wife was on the rocks, and he was despondent. He got hold of a copy of the book, read it, and then read it again. He saw himself in the situations and began to make some course corrections. He was writing to tell me that the changes he was making had markedly improved his relationship with his wife, and they were now planning a commitment ceremony to renew their wedding vows. Now, I'm not sure I planned on my book having quite such a dramatic effect on anyone's life, but I'm awfully glad it helped him turn his marriage around.

Today, there is a growing response to the rudeness and incivility that so characterizes contemporary American life, and it has been expressed from the president on down. Etiquette provides us with a path to civility and positive relationships in all aspects of our lives. Like it did for that young man, etiquette allows each of us to recommit to building a better, more joyful life. And that's not bad for three simple words: consideration, respect, and honesty.

Peter Post
Charlotte, Vermont

They Just Snickered

Just recently I was conducting a seminar for a law firm. The room was filled with fifty participants, most of whom were young associates. I was showing the group the books I would raffle off at the end of the session when I came to a copy of *Essential Manners for Men*. As soon as I announced the title, a hush went over the room and then a soft sound emerged—the sound of fifty voices snickering in unison.

Yes, I know. Men could use manners. And yes, it's really funny thinking that any man would bother to read the book. Yet they did—in numbers great enough that it actually landed on the *New York Times* bestseller list for advice books.

What I've learned after talking to countless men about etiquette is that they really do want information. They want it in a nonjudgmental fashion. They want to hear the ideas and then make up their own minds about what advice they'll adopt. And they need to understand why. Without a "why" behind the advice, they'll never change a behavior.

Surveys in 2002 and 2011

In order to understand what men do well and where they're screwing up, I conducted a survey in 2002 for the first edition and then repeated it in 2011 for the second edition. The surveys focused on daily life, social life, and work life, and most of the questions were the same so as to identify trends over time.

Some issues, such as treating women with respect and the importance of manners, held true over time, while others, like putting the toilet seat down, have clearly changed over the last decade. The chapters that follow will delve into those similarities and differences.

In addition, one sweeping change occurred: Men, especially younger men, are hungry for information that will help them be more successful personally and professionally. I've seen it over and over in the seminars, speeches, and interviews I give, but I didn't have any concrete data to back it up—until now.

While only 14 percent of the respondents in 2002 were men, men made up 46 percent of the 2011 survey. That is a huge shift. Bear in mind that we let the public know about the survey through our monthly newsletter, our Web site, our Facebook page, our Twitter page, and by word of mouth. The majority, if not vast majority, of people we touch this way are women. Yet somehow men found out about the survey, and they responded. Perhaps girlfriends pointed it out to them. Or significant others suggested they take the survey. Frankly, I don't know. What I do know is men responded. And in having those responses, I could look at differing opinions between men and women. Those differences are mentioned throughout the book.

SURVEY SAYS
When You Behave Well, People Notice

To learn more about how people viewed men's behavior, in 2002 we posted four surveys on our Emily Post Institute Web site: daily life, social life, work life, and special occasions. The results of those surveys helped delineate the topics in the first edition. In 2011 we surveyed daily life, social life, and work life again to see what had changed.

Most striking was the increase in the percentage of male respondents. In 2002 only 14 percent were men, while in 2011, 46 percent were men. And 44 percent of the men were twenty to twenty-nine years old.

Young men who responded to the 2011 survey affected the total number of married respondents. In 2002, 66 percent were married but in 2011 that number dropped to 53 percent. Conversely, the number of "Single, never been married" respondents jumped from 16 percent in 2002 to 30 percent in 2011.

For all the variations in gender, age, and marital status, one consistent theme emerged in both sets of surveys: Women want men to treat them with respect, and they notice and value men who have good manners. When a man treats others with respect, his image shines in their eyes.

The 2011 survey also saw an increased emphasis on cleanliness. Women didn't just bash on men, they also let us know what impresses them. Interestingly, men who don't leave a mess and who help clean up got very high marks.

....

It's Not Just Young Men

While on my tour in 2003, I quickly learned the need for the information in this book. One of the first men to buy the book at a signing came up to the table and pulled me aside. "I'm so glad I got here," he said. "I want your book. I'm forty, recently divorced, and now I'm having to get back into the dating game after twenty years of being out of it."

So, men, you're not alone. Men of all ages and in all different stages of relationships are in solidarity with you. They want to know what to do and say so they don't embarrass themselves. They don't want someone telling them what to do, but they do like having someone lay out the options, the possibilities, and then letting them cogitate on it and decide what's best for them.

Funny enough, that's what etiquette really is: understanding what to do and what to expect others to do in return so your focus is on building the relationship.

PART ONE

DAILY LIFE

1

THE "E" WORD

ETIQUETTE IS . . .

G ood. You've made it this far.

Getting past that "E" word is important. Whenever I give a talk, the first thing I do is ask the audience to define "etiquette." Their response is always the same: "Etiquette is a bunch of rules" . . . "Etiquette is the stuff my mother used to make me do" . . . "Etiquette is the old-fashioned way of doing things."

Meanwhile, they're thinking: "Who needs this stuff?"

Emily Post, my great-grandmother, knew what etiquette really was all about. Sure, she wrote a famous etiquette book, which people imagine is filled with rules. And it's true, there *are* a lot of specific guidelines (Emily called them manners) that dictate how people should act in a given situation. But these guidelines exist for a purpose: to help smooth the way for positive interactions between people by prescribing the ways in which we're expected to act and react to people around us.

When we use the manners that are expected of us, the heavens don't part, and crowds don't applaud us; life just goes on smoothly, the way it should. The importance of manners becomes obvious only when we don't use them. For example, one "manner" states that if you say "Hi" or "Good morning" to a person at work, that person should respond in a like manner, since this is the considerate thing to do. So far, so good. But what happens if you said "Hi," and your coworker didn't say anything in return? How would that make you feel? You'd probably wonder something like, "Did I do something to annoy him?" or "Doesn't anybody ever notice that I exist?" or even "Do I smell bad?"

Manners matter. Use them, and you will make the best impression possible.

Still, no one can possibly know all the manners there are or remember precisely how to apply them to every situation. In fact, in today's fast-paced, informal world, manners *don't* always apply in every situation.

Fortunately, the collection of manners that we call etiquette is based on a set of simple but profound principles. Manners and principles are not the same thing: Manners are specific guidelines that change with time and vary across cultures. For instance, children in the United States are taught to shake hands when meeting someone, while Japanese children are taught to greet people by bowing. While the manners themselves may be different, each is correct for that specific culture, and each exists for the same universal reason: to show respect to people when you greet them.

Etiquette is governed by three principles: consideration, respect, and honesty. These provide the framework for defining every manner that has ever been formulated. Each of these principles is timeless. These principles transcend cultural boundaries, cross socioeconomic boundaries, and apply equally to all ages.

CONSIDERATION is understanding how other people and entities are affected by whatever is taking place. Consideration is empathy. It helps us to assess how a situation affects everyone involved, and then act accordingly.

RESPECT is recognizing that how you interact with another person will affect your relationship with that person, and then choosing to take actions that will build relationships rather than injure them. Respect helps us decide how to choose to act toward others.

HONESTY is being truthful, not deceptive. There is a critical difference, too, between benevolent and brutal honesty: "I have a problem with that" vs. "That's a stupid thing to say." Honesty ensures that we act sincerely.

All of the manners discussed in this book and all the solutions to the situations described in these pages involve the application of these three principles.

"But if etiquette is so simple," you ask, "then why are you writing a whole book on the subject?"

In a word: confidence. When men encounter an unfamiliar situation and are unsure what to do, they often either freeze or make the wrong choice. By reading through the situations and examples in this book, you'll learn how to deal graciously and effectively with a wide variety of problems in daily life, social life, and work life. Even more important, you'll gain the knowledge and confidence to resolve such situations on your own whenever they crop up. (If you need further assistance, you can always refer to this book—or dig into *Emily Post's Etiquette*, which addresses every situation under the sun.)

Bottom line: Etiquette isn't about rules, it isn't stuffy, and it's not old-fashioned. Etiquette is a code of treating people with—and making choices based on—consideration, respect, and honesty. When you apply these principles consistently, etiquette becomes a tool that lets you build better relationships and be more successful in every aspect of your life. Etiquette is not about doing what's "correct." Etiquette is about doing what's right.

BEING INCONSIDERATE AND BEING DISRESPECTFUL GO HAND IN HAND

Staring at other women. Talking down to women. Ignoring their opinions. Interrupting. Not introducing them. Simply ignoring them altogether. Walking several steps ahead of a woman rather than beside her. The Post Survey found that women don't simply view these behaviors as being rude or inconsiderate—to women, they represent a fundamental lack of personal respect.

To be fair, most men's inconsiderate or disrespectful behavior is not intentional. Men frequently get lost in their thoughts and go to far-off places in their minds without even realizing the journey has started or considering the consequences. That's when they get into trouble.

Consider the issue of looking at another attractive woman who happens to cross your path. I do this unconsciously, I admit. But when my eyes stop looking at my wife, and my attention shifts away just as she is making an important point, she knows she's lost me. And she's right—my attention has wandered. Whenever a man "switches off" his thinking or wanders off on a mind journey, he runs the risk of looking inconsiderate and, by extension, disrespectful.

On a personal note, it scares me when I see what I've just written because I see some of myself in this description, and unfortunately it's not the good part. How long has it been since I made the bed in the morning? Why didn't I do those dishes that were piled in the sink from last night's dinner? After all, my wife made dinner. The least I could have done was clean up afterward. And I can't remember the last time I bought her flowers. Instead, I've been heard at the supermarket bemoaning the fact that she's picking out flowers and buying them for herself. Talk about clueless!

Now, I'm not *all* bad. I do clean any dishes still left in the sink each morning. I do remember to leave the toilet seat down. And I make coffee every morning and bring it to my wife in bed. In fact, our survey suggests that this last good deed may be the single "little thing" where American men excel the most: It's amazing how many men bring coffee or tea to their significant other in the morning.

Here's the bottom line: Men get it right some of the time, but they don't generally spend enough effort really thinking through how their actions will affect the people around them. And *that's* what good etiquette really is: thinking about what the considerate, respectful thing to do would be, and then doing it. By thinking about our behavior, we turn each action into a conscious choice. The more we practice making those choices, the more often we'll make good choices—and the better our lives and the lives of our loved ones will be.

And that's what makes etiquette worth the effort.

Emily Post on Consideration

Emily Post knew that if you took an imaginary set of scales and balanced all of the rules of etiquette on one side and the principles of consideration, respect, and honesty on the other, the side with the principles would far outweigh the side with the manners.

Here's what she had to say about consideration:

Consideration for the rights and feelings of others is not merely a rule for behavior in public but the very foundation upon which social life is built. The first rule of etiquette—which hundreds of others merely paraphrase or explain or elaborate—is: Never do anything that is unpleasant to others.

2

THE TOP THREE ISSUES
IN DAILY LIFE

The art of etiquette really comes down to being thoughtful of the people you encounter in your everyday life. We all tend to associate "proper behavior" with formal social events—but true etiquette involves behaving with consideration and respect for others in everything that you do, from attending a high-society soiree to simply hanging out around the house.

In fact, daily life is where men tend to run into more trouble than anywhere else. Here's a summary of the three main areas that our female respondents identified as their top hot-button issues when it comes to men and their everyday behavior:

#1: BAD HABITS LEAD THE LIST

At least we're consistent. For all the comments received about annoying behavior, men's bad habits topped the list. These are the things we do, sometimes unconsciously, that are perceived by others as just plain gross. What's interesting is that all the responses citing bad habits focused on seven key behaviors. Men, look in the mirror and see if you recognize any of these habits in yourself (see Chapter 3 for more advice on these topics):

- Adjusting

- Nose picking

- Spitting

- Swearing

- Smoking and chewing tobacco

- Sloppy dressing

- Wearing a hat where they shouldn't

The Undiscussed Effects of Smoking

The smell of smoke and the health implications of secondhand smoke are bad enough. One respondent reminded us of the casual way smokers toss their cigarette butts on the ground. As I write this, annual wildfires are ravaging the west. One butt carelessly tossed out a car window could do immense damage and cost lives. Please, if you've got to smoke, dispose of the butt appropriately and safely.

#2: MAKING A MESS AND NOT HELPING TO CLEAN UP MATTERS—A LOT

Want to drive a woman nuts? Take the dishes to the sink—and then just leave them there. As one of our female respondents put it, "If you can carry them to the sink, why can't you take the time to put them in the dishwasher???"

According to the 2011 Post Survey, men are adept at making a mess. They take dishes to the kitchen and don't wash them; they take food out and then don't put it away. They leave the bathroom sink a mess. They spread newspapers all around and don't pick them up. They leave wet towels on the bed and dirty clothes on the floor. And when they do create the mess, they don't lift a finger to help clean it up.

#3: ACTING IN A SUPERIOR MANNER IS REALLY FRUSTRATING

When men act in a condescending way toward women, women object to it. Men can act as if they are in charge of everything, or they don't listen to a woman's ideas or to what she has to say. This sense of self-importance and need to be the sun of your own solar system is symptomatic of me-ism. It's all about me. Here's how respondents identified a superior attitude in their own words:

"If it's not important to them (men), then it's not important period."

"They have to be right even if they're wrong."

"Fail to ask for help with directions."

"Behavior that implies that whatever he does or wants is more important than what I do or want."

"Placating behavior toward women, as if we're all helpless or ignorant, especially when dealing with an attractive woman."

"Talk to women like they are inferior. We can work on cars, too; just watch me."

"Talk over me. Dominate conversations. Their point of view is the only one that counts."

OTHER ANNOYING BEHAVIORS

Manners Matter

Opening doors. Putting down the toilet seat. Being on time. Not spitting. Taking off your hat indoors. Saying "Please" and "Thank you." Trying to be discreet and quiet when blowing your nose. These and other niceties may seem trivial to many men, but here's the scoop: *It all matters.* When you don't use the manners that people have come to expect—failing to open the door for a woman, for instance—it's not simply a sign that you're clueless; it shows a lack of consideration. *That's* what bothers women about men who don't have manners.

This brings us back to the essential guiding principle of this book: Good manners are not a matter of simply "following the rules." What's important is the reason underlying the desired behavior. Etiquette is about being considerate and honest with others. Manners matter because they are a sign of respect. We hold the door for a woman not because there's a rule that says we should, but because it is an act of kindness and a way to make the woman you're with feel special. When you act in this spirit, she will know it and appreciate you for it. If you hold the door just because "that's the rule," she'll see right through you.

Communication

Dominating the communication comments was a concern that men do not listen well. "They look like they're listening; they may even nod their heads or utter a few 'Uh huhs'; but ask them what you said a few minutes later and they don't remember a thing."

"When they do talk, they tend to focus on the thing that is important to them so it's a monologue rather than a conversation" (see "Acting in a Superior Manner Is Really Frustrating," page 10).

THE TOP THREE MOST IMPRESSIVE THINGS MEN DO IN DAILY LIFE

Before this all sounds like "men do nothing right," it's important to point out that women have a lot of really good things to say about men, too. If you see yourself in these behaviors, great. Pat yourself on the back and keep it up. But if you don't see yourself in one of these behaviors, then consider taking the plunge and trying them out. They've worked for other men and they may work beneficially for you, too.

Be Responsible and Respectful

The underlying goal of being respectful and responsible is to treat your significant other like an equal but not like one of the guys. You love her, you care for her, you share your life with her. So focus on the qualities that engender those emotions in you and then let her know by talking positively about her.

Be appreciative. She does a lot for you. The simplest words to say, when said sincerely, can make her warm inside with good feelings toward you: "Thank you."

Over and over again, women acknowledged the respect they have for their significant other's role in providing financial security for the family. But it's not just the financial responsibility. It's also the ability to share the workload and the motivation to get things done without being nagged at.

Finally, the respectful man is confident and understanding enough to take responsibility for his actions and be willing to apologize for his frustrating or annoying behaviors. Things can and will go wrong and when they do the first step to recovery is saying "I'm sorry."

Act Chivalrous

It really is the little things in life that matter. Men, take note: Women notice when you make an effort on their behalf, and they really like it. Open doors, hold a chair, let a woman walk in first, offer an arm to hold, walk on the outer side of the sidewalk, help her with her coat, stand up to greet her, carry a heavy load for her, offer the seat to her on public transportation, carry the groceries. Do those chivalrous actions not just for your significant other, but for colleagues, friends, and even strangers. It shows that you believe they are the right things to do and not just a way to impress her.

Oh, and did I mention holding doors? Because they did. A lot. More than anything else, holding doors was cited as one of the most impressive behaviors displayed by men.

Help with Chores

Women are impressed when men do their chores. And that makes sense because doing chores is an important part of building a life together. So when you do your chores, you're not just getting the work done, you're showing your commitment to your relationship.

The best part of doing chores is, in many cases, that you end up getting to do what you want to do while also getting credit for it. I love to cook, especially on the grill. So I cook, not every meal, but regularly. And not just the meat. I grill the vegetables and prepare the whole meal. This gives my wife a break from her jampacked day, and I look great in her eyes.

3

OTHER HOT SPOTS

The key to a peaceful, happy home life is to pay special attention to the "hot spots" that tend to crop up on any given day. In the 2011 Post Survey, women expressed an overwhelming sense of frustration about how clueless men can be. All too often, we men are simply not aware of how our actions affect the people around us, and at times we seem to get into an altered mind state.

Fortunately, etiquette provides a roadmap back to reality when our minds wander. It gives us a set of clues for building solid, respectful relationships—and whenever you share a living space with others, you are, in fact, in a relationship, since everything you do affects them as well. What these other people generally want is for you to respect them and the efforts they are making to keep the space livable, and to contribute a like amount of effort yourself.

SEEING THE MAN IN THE MIRROR

Mud season in Vermont is a vile time of year. It makes sense that a typical rule in our home is "Wipe your feet before coming into the house." But the fact is, *it really doesn't matter* if I wipe my feet when I come inside with muddy boots on. What matters is that I notice the muddy trail I've made and then clean it up. When I do this, I'm being considerate and aware of how my actions affect someone else—namely my wife, who cleaned the floor and would like it to stay clean. If I choose not to wipe my feet every time I enter the house, so be it—provided I also take responsibility for cleaning up the mess I've made.

My muddy boots are a metaphor for a larger truth: By holding up a mirror to my own behavior, I am able to turn a potentially difficult situation into a no-brainer. We all have to learn to keep one eye on this mental mirror and see ourselves as others see us. This means being conscious at all times of how our actions affect others.

Sharing the Load

Congratulations! In the Post surveys, we men get high marks for mowing the lawn. But there must be any number of men who view this chore as making up their entire 50-percent contribution to the job of running the household. The problem is, there's a lot more to managing a house than mowing the lawn. Here are just some of the other daily chores respondents cited:

Laundry

Housework

Ironing

Watching the baby

Cooking

Making the bed(s)

Vacuuming

Taking out the garbage

Changing lightbulbs

Doing the grocery shopping

Paying the bills

Planning an evening out

....

Planning an Evening Out
....

Our surveys received reams of comments about how men never lift a finger to figure out what the couple is going to do on a date. All I know is that when I plan a date with my wife, it has a superb effect on her.

Recently, we went on a cruise with her entire family. It really turned out great—despite what you're thinking. The cruise departed from New York City at 2:00 P.M. on a Saturday afternoon. Plotting with my wife's older brother, I found a low-cost airfare from Burlington to New York and got tickets to a fabulous Broadway play for the Friday night before our departure. We had a great dinner before the show, and even managed a limo ride back to her brother's house afterward. Admittedly, that's a pretty extravagant date—but it was a great evening and all she had to do was be there and enjoy.

On other occasions, I'll suggest we eat out—and then call the restaurant to make a reservation. If I also arranged for the sitter, that was the absolute icing on the cake.

....

When it comes to chores around the house, very often we'll identify something specific we want to get done together. We might spend Saturday morning weeding the vegetable garden or repainting the front hall or cleaning out the refrigerator (it's frightening that our fridge can get so bad it takes a whole morning to clean it out). That leaves Saturday afternoon for golf, skiing, or another activity we can share. The key is that we tackle the chore together, and we plan something fun to do afterward. That way, no one feels that they're left doing all the dirty work.

"What TV Show Are We Going to Watch?"

One survey respondent defined this problem as "Lifetime versus SportsCenter." Another woman wrote, "Most people can only watch a John Wayne flick so many times." (Personally I disagree; I have yet to tire of watching the Duke.)

Just the other night, my wife and I were channel surfing the movies. "Debbie says that's a good movie," my wife announced suddenly when *27 Dresses* popped up as one of the selections. "It's a chick flick," she added, and we passed it by without further comment.

The way our arrangement works, there are "her" shows, "my" shows, and "our" shows. Someday in the near future I'll be either on the road or at a hockey game, and she can catch *27 Dresses* then. The same goes for me: I'll save *Fort Apache* for sometime when my wife is either out or not interested in watching. Even if you don't have a satellite system or cable that repeats the show over and over again, the key is to recognize it's "our" house and "our" living room—and that we both need to compromise when watching "our" television together.

Share the Remote?

The second most difficult conflict caused by the TV involves the ownership of the remote control. I have a good friend who literally keeps the remotes tied next to "his" recliner in the living room. Ostensibly this is to prevent the dreaded misplacement of the remote, but it also places the clicker conveniently under his control.

I think my wife wonders whether I simply use the remote to see how fast I can click through the channels. As any true remote control junkie knows, if you click fast enough you can actually watch two or three shows simultaneously. How your viewing partner feels about watching this sort of triple feature is another matter.

Lately, I've been learning to slow down or, better yet—horror of horrors for anyone with a pathological need to control the remote—even offer my wife the clicker on occasion.

"Here, honey, you find something," I say as sweetly as I can.

"No, no, no," she always replies, pushing it away as if it's cursed.

This is admittedly a risky strategy, because you've got to be prepared for those times when the other person actually does take control. The upside is that this approach puts a stop to any arguing about the remote.

The bottom line: Television viewing should be relaxing for everyone. To keep it from becoming adversarial, think before you act and be considerate by taking everyone's interests into account.

THE TELEPHONE

The telephone is a diabolical technological invention. You can't live without it, but you can't succeed with it—at least, not if you believe what the Post survey respondents have to say about the phone. For them, misuse of the telephone falls into three very clear-cut categories: not answering the phone, not using the phone, and failing to take messages.

Not Answering the Phone

It's the stuff of television sitcoms. Scene: The male character is lounging on the couch, watching something on TV, when the phone rings. The phone is usually about ten feet away.

"Honey, can you get that?" the man shouts.

Honey trudges up the basement stairs carrying a load of laundry and, huffing and puffing, answers the phone. "Keep it down, will you?" her husband yells. "I'm trying to watch the game here."

Unfortunately, TV sitcoms often parody real life.

Bottom line: When the phone rings, answer it.

Not Using the Phone

Typically, problems with the phone are associated with the abuse of using it. But men have mastered a whole other side of phone misbehavior: not using it at the most inappropriate times.

"Call me if you're going to be late," my wife would ask as I got ready to head out the door on the way to work. She may be trying to time dinner so it'll be ready when I get home. Or she may have errands, work, or children's events to coordinate. Or she may simply worry that something has happened to me if I don't arrive when I'm expected.

It seems like a reasonable request. The problem is, I have failed to make that call a few thousand times. Even with my cell phone, which you'd think would solve the problem, I was still guilty of not calling. Worse yet, I might not check it to see if she wanted me to stop and pick up something at the market. I'm working on it. Now, at least, I fire off a text "On my way home" before I start the car.

Peace.

Not Taking Messages

Taking messages can be a pain in the neck. Let's say I'm up to my elbows in sawdust, working on a project in my shop. My wife isn't home. The kids aren't home. The phone rings. Now, I'm no good at letting it go to voice mail. Technology has defeated me: I must answer that phone.

It's for my wife. "I'll let her know you called," I promise, dropping the phone into its cradle and rushing back downstairs to finish marking the wood for the next cut. Measure twice, cut once. I'm completely focused on my project.

Sure, I'll remember to tell her about the call. And it snows in July in Vermont occasionally, too.

In the grand scheme of things—such as world peace or solving the problems of starvation and overpopulation—actions like taking a phone message don't seem all that important. The fact is, however, etiquette isn't about momentous acts. It is about smoothing the way through life for ourselves and the people around us.

That's why taking a message becomes important. It's one act in a continuum of actions that cumulatively make a difference. By doing it and doing it well, we are able to reach out and help another person.

So in spite of my annoyance at the interruption, I grab a piece of paper and jot the message down: name, number, time of call, and the message.

PASSING GAS

Burping and farting: It's remarkable how often these came up in all three 2011 Post surveys. While both are bodily functions that sometimes escape without warning, for the most part, it's possible to delay the inevitable until you move away or retire to a restroom. With burps, while it can be fun to let one out with a rumble that rivals the sound of a train roaring past you, the reality is you can almost always burp noiselessly without calling attention to yourself.

SCRATCHING WHAT ITCHES

If you have an itch, scratch it—right?

Well, that works for your nose. But the Post Survey found that a great many women can't understand why guys need to scratch and adjust their "privates" so often. As we men know, there's usually a darn good reason: Either you have an itch, or your privates shifted into the wrong place and need to be rearranged.

The real issue, however, is how to "adjust" yourself in a way that doesn't offend the people around you. For example, the "full frontal adjust" is throwing the whole matter in the face of any woman who happens to be nearby—and she is not going to be impressed. Instead, if you need to adjust yourself, turn away discreetly before making the "grab and move." If you do this maneuver properly, no one will even be aware of what you're doing.

"But," you say to me, "I don't even realize I'm doing it."

Then start realizing. If you've got to sneeze, you turn away so you don't spray the people around you, right? The same applies to scratching yourself: Being considerate means being conscious of what you're doing—and how it affects the people around you.

ATTIRE

The clothing we choose to wear makes such a strong statement to others even if we can't read that statement ourselves. Usually that statement is something like "What a slob" or "How disrespectful."

What's interesting is for every complaint about dress, women equally praised men who make an effort to wear the right clothing at the right time: in other words dressing for the occasion. Even something as innocuous as going to the movies can be an opportunity for a man to make a great impression. A quick shave, a run through the shower, a clean shirt and slacks, and she's going to be beaming. Try it. You'll see.

HYGIENE

This is the one time I'm going to mention it: Body odor, bad breath, and poor grooming take so little time to correct, yet when corrected they have such a positive effect on everyone in your life.

Now comes the hard part. How can you tell if you have body odor or bad breath, or if you're using too much cologne, or your antiperspirant really smells worse than nothing at all? You can't judge these things for yourself because you're too familiar with the smells to notice them. The problem is that if you *are* an offender, most people are far too uncomfortable about the subject to ever bring it up on their own.

This is a shame, because at heart we're all begging to be apprised of the truth. In my seminars, I always ask, "How many people here would prefer it if a friend tells you if you have body odor or bad breath?" Whenever I pose this question, virtually every hand in the room goes up.

Fortunately, there's a solution to this dilemma: Place a friendly inquiry with a friend, a roommate, your spouse, or your significant other. If you ask them, then they have permission to speak. "Tom, I gotta ask you something and it may sound strange, but I need to know. Do I have bad breath? Because if I do, I want to do something about it."

If you don't have bad breath, Tom simply says so. End of story. If you *do* have bad breath, he will almost certainly feel relieved at finally being able to say something without having to be the one who brought it up.

Some men are selective about their hygiene habits: They allow themselves to go unwashed or have bad breath at home, but not when they go out. Keep in mind, there's no etiquette rule that says it's okay to drop your standards at home.

ETIQUETTE IMPERATIVE
Wash Your Hands

Wash after you use the bathroom, *every time.*

PET PROBLEMS

Pets really are wonderful companions, but they can be terrible for the neighbors. A dog that barks incessantly can drive your neighbor crazy.

It's important to keep your pet under control at all times. You may think it's cute that your dog does the rounds of the neighborhood—cute, that is, until you get a call from a frustrated neighbor whose garbage has been torn open and spread all across his lawn by Fido. If the neighbors complain about your pet's barking or wandering or digging, talk with your vet about possible solutions.

It goes almost without saying that an aggressive dog has to be kept under tight control. Even the sweetest, tamest looking dog, can, under certain circumstances, bare its teeth and suddenly look very menacing. If this is your dog, you may not be able to let him out unless he's under your supervision.

WHEN YOU'RE NOT THE PROBLEM

Now, maybe you're thinking to yourself, "None of this advice so far applies to *me!*"

Okay, let's suppose you're the type of thoughtful person who never fails to clean the sink or pick up your dirty clothes. In fact, you're fastidious—it's the other person who is the problem. In this case, you have two options.

Option Number One

Do nothing. Particularly with a wife or live-in significant other, this is often the best policy. Example: Throughout thirty-nine years of marriage, my wife has buried the armchair in our bedroom under her clothes. It's been so well covered for so long that I no longer have any clear idea of the color of the chair's fabric. Now, I'm no neatfreak. Anyone who has ever seen my office knows this. But somehow I've developed the habit of putting my dirty clothes in the hamper every morning, and putting away my other clothes in the bureau or the closet. (Actually I do this primarily out of self-interest: We've divided chores and my wife does the laundry—

so by making sure my clothes are where they are meant to be, I'm ensuring that they get cleaned.)

Anyway, the one thing I don't *ever* do is say a word to my wife about the pile of clothes on the chair. This is simply not an issue I care to expend any built-up goodwill capital on. Besides, the upholstery has lasted an incredibly long time—no doubt due to the fact that the chair gets virtually no use and no light can shine through to fade the fabric. Here's to the chair: May it last another thirty-nine years!

Option Number Two

Try to change your housemate's offending behavior. This is tricky work, to say the least. Any time you talk to someone about what you perceive to be their failings, they tend to become very defensive very quickly. Before you pursue this option, go back and carefully reconsider Option Number One. Ask yourself: Is this issue *really* worth stirring the pot over?

If you do decide to plunge ahead with your behavior modification project, remember that your goal in attempting to change someone else's behavior should always be to build a better relationship with that person, not simply to be critical for its own sake.

4

TWO ROOMS THAT CAN MAKE OR BREAK YOUR HOME LIFE

Remember that day when you moved into the first place of your own? You were the king of your castle: nobody to answer to, nobody to share chores with. You could watch the TV shows you wanted to watch, eat the foods you wanted to eat, and clean up or not. What a great setup!

It's also usually a very temporary state of affairs. One day—sooner than they might have imagined—most men wake up to find themselves married or living with a significant other or roommate. And whenever living space is shared, differences of opinion inevitably arise over the care and use of those spaces. These differences can turn into conflicts if not handled thoughtfully.

Fortunately, the complexities of thoughtful home sharing can be vastly simplified by thinking of your house as a series of discrete spaces—each with its own set of issues. Keep these key issues firmly in mind, and life will be blissfully peaceful on the home front.

In both our Post surveys, we asked which shared spaces have the most potential to cause conflicts. Two rooms topped the list: the kitchen and the bathroom. Let's consider each in turn.

CLEAN KITCHEN, WARM HEART

When we asked women to identify the leading cause of conflict in the kitchen, they gave one overwhelming answer: Men don't do their share when it comes to cleaning up, especially after themselves.

I admit to being a primary offender in this regard. I used to drive my wife nuts on Saturday afternoons: I'd wander into the kitchen, and out would come all the fixings for a delectable Dagwood sandwich. The problem was, after making my sandwich, I wanted to eat it then and there. I'd sit right down at the kitchen table or, worse still, carry my creation into the living room to watch TV and munch away.

After a few minutes of this, my wife would wander in and invariably ask the same question: Why couldn't I clean up my mess *before* eating my sandwich?

The answer seemed obvious to me. "After all that work to make the sandwich, I want to eat it now," I would point out *reasonably*.

"What about the mess in the kitchen?"

Oh, that. "I'll get to it during halftime or whatever," I'd mumble, guiltily tucking back into my sandwich.

In my interviews and speeches about etiquette, I talk quite a bit about how sincerity is an integral component in building relationships. Looking back on this particular scenario, I realize now that my sincerity quotient was in the cellar. My wife had seen those sandwich fixings stay out on the counter time and again. She knew (and, deep down, so did I) that I was only kidding myself; I would never get around to cleaning up my mess, and she was going to end up doing it instead.

Then, one Saturday, I had a breakthrough moment. Maybe the above scene had finally been repeated one too many times, or maybe the game of the week just wasn't very appealing that day—but for some reason, as I was making my sandwich in my usual fashion (as fast as possible, so I could get in front of the TV before the game started), the memory of my wife's words somehow penetrated my food- and football-fixated mind. To my own amazement, I actually stopped dead in my tracks and *put all the sandwich fixings away before I started to eat.*

Of course, my sandwich is a metaphor for all of the important activity that goes on in a kitchen. The kitchen really is the soul of the home. It's where the family's meals are prepared and often eaten. It's the room that requires the most cooperation to keep it clean and functioning.

ETIQUETTE IMPERATIVE
Making Promises, Keeping Promises

"Honey, there's just five minutes left. Let me just finish watching this show. Then I'll help you." You've made a promise. Now it's time to abide by it. The fact that another ball game is just starting on another channel doesn't relieve you from the promise.

Sincerity matters. If you say you'll clean the dishes, then do it. Forgetting sets a pattern, and it establishes a precedent that your word isn't good. In any relationship, the trust that grows out of keeping your promises is a cornerstone of its success.

When it comes to holding up your end of the kitchen duties, there are three simple keys:

1. *Pitch in consistently to clean up any general mess that accumulates.* This applies to cleaning up after meals, and also putting away all the junk that simply piles up during the day: groceries, mail, coats, boots, hats, gloves, and shoes. Somehow this stuff seems to grow on its own in the kitchen.

2. *Take personal responsibility for your own mess.* When you make or do anything that involves food or any other kitchen supplies— like my Dagwood sandwich—*clean it up as soon as possible.*

3. *Complete all kitchen chores.* Men often think that where kitchen chores are concerned, half a loaf is better than none. I'm as guilty as the next guy: I would much rather leave the just-washed dinner dishes dripping in the dish rack than dry them and put them away. Now that I've learned to put the fixings and dishes away, I have one more step to master: closing the cupboard doors after I've opened them. Once you've started a job, *finish it.*

Make the Bedroom a "Safe Zone"

Interestingly, while other rooms seem to be rife with issues, many survey respondents described their bedrooms as a "safe zone"—a place where couples consciously agree to leave their arguments behind. Instead, it's reserved as a space where they can share intimacy and be safe in their togetherness.

"Fortunately, we don't have problems here," wrote one respondent. "We both respect each other's space, and we usually enjoy spending time in this room."

"Never fight in the bedroom," added another. "It sours the sex." A third survey taker reported, "No problems in the bedroom. It is as if it is a restful sanctuary, and we respect that."

I like that concept—respect for the space and respect for each other within the space. Not that the bedroom is completely issue-free, of course. Snoring, blanket hogging, cranking up the volume on the television, not helping to make the bed, and lack of personal hygiene came up repeatedly in the Post Survey as behaviors that can lead to conflict in the bedroom. One sin of omission took the cake, however: leaving dirty clothes around. So remember, to keep harmony in your bedroom, put your dirty clothes where they belong—in the clothes hamper. Better yet, learn how to operate that washer and dryer or take a load to the laundromat yourself. Her gratitude will know no bounds.

THE BATTLE OF THE BATHROOM

The bathroom is the one place where we all truly want to be private and comfortable. In an ideal world, everyone would have a bathroom that was theirs and theirs alone. In reality, however, most of us share a bathroom with a significant other, and perhaps with other family members or roommates. This overlap of personal space is where trouble starts.

For men, the most important thing to understand is that women tend to be very particular about the bathroom. Not only did they comment far more often than men about the bathroom, their comments were very pointed, to say the least. They got down and dirty about everything from missed aim to shaving stubble in the sink to wet towels on the floor and toothpaste all over the counter. This leads to a major truth that men are best off simply accepting: The bathroom is her domain. One man responded about the bathroom, "Like the kitchen, it's all her space, she just loans you some of it." You, the man, are essentially a visitor. If you don't believe me, just look at the "stuff" in your own bathroom. In my case, my "stuff" takes up part of one drawer. Hers takes up the rest of the room.

That's why, when it comes to bathroom behavior, it's almost always a good idea to be accommodating of your partner's needs and desires. This delicate area is generally not the place to make a stand on some point of personal self-expression.

In 2002, the toilet seat screamed out from the Post Survey as the number one frustration women had in the bathroom. Interestingly, men seem to have taken note. In the 2011 Post Survey, the toilet seat ranked fifth in the list of annoying behaviors. Other annoying bathroom behaviors included leaving it messy, not cleaning up, problems with it as a shared space, and hair left in the sink or tub.

The Mess and Cleaning Up

Whether it's hair or stubble or shaving cream or toothpaste, we men seem to take no notice of the trail of destruction we leave in our wakes. Perhaps that's because we're used to having our significant other follow behind and clean our mess so it's up to her standard. But as we've seen above, it's not our forgetful standard that matters. This is her room, and we should respect it and leave it for her the way she wants it.

The Sink

One of the problems with shaving is that it's messy, especially if you use shaving cream and a manual razor. When I got married, I quickly realized that even though I might not be bothered by that stubble in the sink, my wife did not share my view.

As a visitor to this room, it's your job to learn how to leave the sink— and the rest of the bathroom—in a condition suitable to the owner of the room. One easy way for me to avoid my wife's wrath is to spend a minute or so making sure the sink is cleaned of my shaving residue and ready for her use. I know that I'm not going to get rewarded, praised, or even acknowledged for this act—but that's not why I do it. I do it because I know she doesn't like it when she goes to use the sink and finds it full of my stubble.

In other words, it's the considerate thing to do.

One final sink tip: After I shave, there's always water left on the counter. I make sure I wipe this water up and leave the counter dry. Why? Because one day, when I didn't wipe it up, my wife came in after me and leaned against the counter so she could get a better look at herself in the mirror while she did her makeup. When she stepped away from the sink, her nice white skirt had a big wet spot on it.

I only made that mistake once.

The Bathtub/Shower

Bathtubs conjure up all sorts of sexy images: bubbles; an adventurous moment with your significant other or someone you're dreaming of; feet, legs, arms, hands all intertwined. It gets pretty good.

Dream on. I don't know about your setup, but our tub is five feet long, tops. If I ever did try to climb in with my wife, the faucet would leave a permanent impression on my back. Save that cuddling-in-the-bubble-bath stuff for your vacations in that hotel room with the tub as big as the Ritz. When it comes to the typical bathtub in the home, your thoughts should be confined to how you can keep it clean and attractive for your wife or girlfriend. I doubt that a roommate would want to clean up your mess either.

Hair in the Sink or Tub

Whether you have a stall shower or a bathtub that also doubles as a shower, have you noticed how the water often starts building up in the tub or stall while you're taking a shower? That slow-draining water is a clear indication that hair and soap scum are partially blocking the drain. This not only forces you and your partner to shower in ankle-deep water, but also leaves behind a dirty ring in a tub. The proper (and considerate) response is to grab a paper towel or tissue and clear the drain, then grab a sponge and some cleanser and make that bathtub ring disappear. (A consistently sluggish drain may be a sign that the trap is clogged as well, meaning that a superficial cleaning won't help. In this case, try some liquid drain cleaner. If that fails, it's time to grab your tool kit and give the trap a cleaning, or bite the bullet and call a plumber.)

"But it's mostly *her* hair," you argue. It doesn't matter. Just clean out the drain. You were the last one in the shower, so you own the problem, whether it's your fault or not.

Sharing Space

This issue stood out from the pack in our 2011 Survey. The people with no problems sharing space are the people with two separate bathrooms. Unfortunately, most of us aren't in that lucky position. So we've got to figure out how to share so we're not bumping elbows.

With only one sink, my wife and I have learned a valuable lesson: We need to communicate before we start getting ready. "Why don't I shave while you shower and then when you get out, the sink is all yours," I'll suggest. If she's amenable, great. It seems like a good plan because drying her hair will take a relatively long time, so if she gets a jump on it, we're more likely to both be ready at the same time.

Shared space also means identifying whose stuff goes where and then respecting that division at all times. Recognize that she will probably have more "stuff," and she'll spend far more time in the bathroom than you, so give her the space she'll need for her things. It'll be worth it to you in the long run.

A Delicate Subject

Let's just put it right on the table: smell. Face it, it happens to all of us. And when it does, it's usually much less noticeable to us than to someone else who enters this shared space. If your bathroom doesn't have an air freshener, get one and then use it. If your bathroom has a fan, turn it on. You'll both be happier.

The Toilet Seat

We now come to the all-important issue of the toilet seat. Here's the scenario: It's three in the morning, and your dream's been pretty good. But now you're awake, and you realize that you really need to use the bathroom.

You carefully slip out of bed—woe to you if you wake her—and head into the bathroom with one thought: to get your business done and get back to bed. The problem is that now, at the ungodly hour of 3:00 A.M., you are facing a crucial etiquette challenge: the toilet seat.

Here are the two transgressions you can make in this befuddled state, in order of their seriousness:

TRANSGRESSION 1—You lift the toilet seat, do your business, and then pad back to bed without putting the seat back down. Maybe you just forgot. Or maybe you were feeling a little lazy. "It's only fair," you think to yourself. "I raised the seat—she can lower it."

Wrong. This issue has nothing to do with division of labor. When nature calls at an ungodly hour and a woman settles sleepily into a sitting position, *she expects that seat to be down.* Anything other than that is a very rude surprise. Think about it: Would you like to sit on the rim? Or worse, fall in?

TRANSGRESSION 2—You forget to put the seat up *before* relieving yourself. Remember, it's dark, you're sleepy, and even at high noon your aim isn't always perfectly true. If that seat isn't dry and clean as a whistle and your wife rises and heads to *the same toilet,* frankly, I can think of many other places I'd rather be.

Of course, you *know* the right thing to do in both situations. But merely *knowing* isn't enough. There are some tasks that men are absolutely required to perform in order to make life easier and more trouble-free for everyone. This is one of them. Sometimes avoiding trouble is the best reason of all for doing the right thing.

Toilet Paper

No one should have to face this sort of thing first thing in the morning: Only two or three sheets were left on the roll. No spare was in sight and my wife was blissfully asleep.

We all know what it feels like to be in that situation. As men, we should always make a point of knowing where the spare roll of toilet paper is kept and bringing that spare roll within arm's reach whenever the current roll starts running low. (Many households keep a spare roll nearby at all times, under a cover or in some other convenient container.)

Even better: When the roll actually runs out, don't rely on your wife to pop the new roll into the dispenser but play the unsung hero and do it yourself.

Privacy

The subject of bathroom privacy is more delicate and somewhat more abstract than other bathroom etiquette issues, but it's no less important. When you're living alone, you can leave the door open while you do whatever is necessary, and it won't change the universe one bit. Once you begin living in a shared space, however, a closed door becomes important. This is true when you are using the bathroom yourself, and even more true when your partner is using it. A closed door is an unspoken request for privacy, and it should be honored at all times.

5

How Others View Us

My typical Saturday morning goes something like this: The sun is shining, the lawn needs mowing, the oil in my car has to be changed, and there are ten other chores that need attention after that. In this situation, I often don't shower or shave. I just throw on a T-shirt and jeans, and I'm ready for the day.

What I'm saying is that it's okay to be a little grubby on Saturday mornings—as long as you're tinkering on your own, or running errands to the hardware store or the grocery store. But this permissiveness has its limits: When the phone rings and friends ask us to join them for lunch, I know I'm going to have to hit the shower, shave, and put on some clean clothes. The same holds true if my wife says, "Peter, let's go to the movies later," or if the dinner hour rolls around and I'm still immersed in chores. There's no question that I've got to be cleaned up: shaved, combed, dressed nicely, and smelling good by the time we leave the house or sit down at the dinner table.

Friends, Foes, and the Baseball Cap

In the Middle Ages, knights in shining armor met each other encased from head to toe in metal. Often they simply could not be identified and had no idea if the other knight was friend or foe. So they took to lifting off their helmets to reveal their identities to each other. The servers at banquets in the Middle Ages were required to remove their hats as a mark of deference to the patrons. The removing of a head covering became a custom and evolved into the removal of a hat being a mark of respect. This action has remained a custom ever since.

When you enter a person's home, removing your hat is a symbol of your respect for the owner. Likewise, as you enter a restaurant, taking off your cap is the right thing to do for the people you are with and for the other diners. Anytime you enter a place of worship, your baseball cap should come off. However, when you enter a store or other public space, you can keep your cap on.

Each of us is responsible for the image we project. Taking that responsibility seriously is a clear signal of your respect for others. If you choose to go on a date without cleaning up first, you are responsible when your date decides she doesn't want to see you again. Pass gas or let loose with a string of expletives when you're with a group of friends, and they may forgive one episode—but make it a habit, and you could quickly find yourself without friends.

I didn't pick these examples at random. We asked our 2011 survey respondents to tell us where men are most likely to have significant problems with their appearance. Failing to bathe, passing gas, and foul language all emerged as major issues—as did smoking, chewing gum, and spitting.

SURVEY SAYS
What Women Really Think About Men and Grooming

"Clean hair and nails are a must; a well-groomed man is very sexy!"

"They have a lack of personal hygiene—especially ear hair or nose hair."

"Soap and water are cheap enough for everyone to be clean."

"How come men get away with not shaving for days?"

"Smelling of stale smoke on clothing and breath."

"Teeth and hair are very important; if you can't take care of your own teeth, I can't imagine what else you must not be taking care of."

SMOKING

It used to be a smoker's world. You could light up just about anywhere—in an airplane, in a cab, at a restaurant, in a store, or in a person's home—with total freedom.

Not anymore. Nobody is impressed with a person who smokes where smoking is prohibited. When you visit another person's home, never light up inside without asking permission first—and be prepared to step outside good-naturedly for your smoke if your host requests it.

The smell of smoke on your clothes or in your car can be bothersome to others. Imagine spiffing yourself up for a hot date, cologne and all—then having a smoke before picking up your date. Greeting her with the aroma of tobacco clinging to you will be counterproductive, to say the least!

Cigar Smoking

Sometimes, especially when cigars are involved, men forget that their exhaled smoke is generally viewed as obnoxious, invasive, and annoying. It's worth remembering that many people have an especially visceral reaction to cigar smoke.

If you do choose to light up a stogie in a private home or a public place that allows it, check with everyone in your group first to make sure no one minds—then offer cigars to anyone who wants one, including the women.

Don't forget that cigar smoke can linger in your clothes. I make sure to leave my sweater or jacket outside to air out.

CHEWING GUM

My good friend Becky was severely grossed out the other day. She was working the circuit at her gym, moving from one station to the next, when she saw it: There on the bench, where she was about to sit, was a sticky wad of chewing gum.

You have to wonder what goes through some people's minds.

Chewing gum is appropriate only when you can do it without negatively affecting the people around you. Making cracking sounds, chewing it with your mouth open, or blowing bubbles are all revolting intrusions on the people around you. Chew your gum silently with your mouth closed if you must chew at all. And when you're on a date—whether it's a first date or a night out with your spouse or significant other—forget the gum completely.

SPITTING

Most men are pretty adept at spitting. In junior high, we used to have contests to see who could spit the farthest. Of course, back then, we also didn't worry too much about what the girls thought. Today, in adulthood, it's different. And women put spitting high on the list of things men do that truly annoy them.

To be sure, there's a difference between spitting on an athletic field and letting fly as you're walking arm-in-arm with your date. The trick is to avoid allowing your behavior when you're alone, on the athletic field, or hanging out with the guys turn into a habitual action that you do without thinking, even when you are with a woman or in polite company.

For starters, when you're with other people and need to clear your throat, excuse yourself and take care of your business in private. If you can't excuse yourself, discreetly spit into a paper tissue and dispose of it.

WHO CUT THE CHEESE?

Another rite of passage for adolescent boys is learning how to pass gas for maximum effect. While this talent might have wowed your thirteen-year-old buddies, it will not impress the adults around you—particularly the women. In our 2011 Post Survey, one out of six respondents indicated that passing gas was one of the "things men do that really annoy women."

What do you do if you're on a date and you've got to pass gas?

My answer: What do you do if you have to go to the bathroom? The principle is the same. You can retire briefly to the bathroom or hold it in. If for some reason you absolutely can't excuse yourself and you can't hold it any longer, then let it pass as discreetly as possible—and be prepared to own up and apologize, if necessary.

SWEARING

Basically, swearing is a cultural issue. Certain groups may be comfortable with the use of certain words, while other groups may find the same words offensive. For example, I was recently asked to do a seminar for a national company with two distinct cultures—a southern culture and a northeast culture. The firm's northeast workers have a habit of swearing in their business conversations, while the southern employees never use profanity. As a result, the Southerners feel very uncomfortable when talking to their northeast colleagues.

People also have different opinions about what constitutes swearing. That's why I always try to keep colorful language out of my presentations; I don't want to risk offending any participants, and the use of swear words isn't going to enhance my message one bit.

Bottom line: Being careful to choose our words so we don't offend our listeners is a lesson we all need to relearn periodically. Even when you're with a group of friends accustomed to using profanity, if you think that someone—anyone—in the group might be bothered by it, then be considerate and hold your tongue. And if you're not sure . . . hold it anyway.

ETIQUETTE IMPERATIVE
Swearing Boomerangs Back on You

Curb your swearing, especially around kids. When you swear, children learn from your behavior. If it's okay for you to do it, then they think it's okay for them to do it.

WOMEN SWEAR AND MEN GOSSIP

Just like we think men are the only gender that swears, we also think that women are the only gender that gossips. Well, it ain't so. Women swear and men gossip.

In fact, I'm amazed at how much men gossip. If you could listen to a foursome walking down a fairway, their conversation breaks down into a few well-defined categories: jokes, sports, and gossip. Unfortunately, gossip is insidious. Unlike a joke, which is a momentary thing, gossip lingers. It clouds our opinion of the people being gossiped about.

So, whether it's on the golf course, at the water cooler, or over lunch, make the effort to put a stop to gossip when you hear it. At the very least don't contribute to it and don't repeat what you hear. A more proactive stance would include indicating you're uncomfortable with the conversation, offering a defense of the individual, and refusing to be a party to the conversation by excusing yourself. When men refuse to be part of gossip and make the proactive effort, women notice their willingness to stand up for another person, and they appreciate it.

6

A MAN AND HIS CAR

It's 5:45 P.M., the end of a long day, and I'm glad to be on the way home. Country roads in Vermont are beautiful, and I'm looking forward to a relaxing drive. Then I see it—a drab, ten-year-old sedan, crawling along the road in front of me. The speed limit is a mere thirty-five miles per hour, and this guy's barely doing thirty. Traffic's coming the other way, and I'm trapped: I have to brake.

I'm so close I can't see the road between me and him, and I can feel the rush of adrenaline. *"Come on, idiot, move it!"* I snarl to myself. After a couple of minutes of this, believe it or not, he starts *slowing down.* Meanwhile my blood pressure is moving just as quickly in the opposite direction. A right turn's coming up, we're down to ten miles per hour, and I'm boiling over with impatience. Just as he starts to turn, he finally switches on his blinker.

I squeeze by, hit the accelerator, and roar past his receding rear end, thinking, *"That showed him."* A mile later I turn onto the dirt road where I live, and before I know it I'm home—still hyped from the adrenaline rush from my encounter.

I wasn't as bad as I might have been—after all, I didn't yell, curse (not so the driver could hear me anyway), or worse. Still, with the benefit of hindsight, I can count several aggressive behaviors in my one brief encounter: tailgating, unnecessarily abrupt speed change, lost temper, and venting my frustration verbally.

Road rage, aggressive behavior—call it what you will—is dangerous, foolish, and doesn't get you anywhere. As it turns out, I got home one or two minutes later than I would have otherwise. Big deal. If I had simply taken a few deep breaths and kept calm instead of overreacting, I would have arrived home relaxed and in a good mood rather than tense and fuming.

While you're never going to be able to control how others act in their cars, you can start changing your own road rage behavior. The first essential step is to recognize that you're engaging in this type of behavior. Ask yourself these questions:

- Am I screaming at other drivers?

- Am I *always* right and the other driver *always* wrong?

- Do I sense that my blood pressure is rising rapidly during a frustrating encounter on the road?

- Do I think of my vehicle as a weapon of revenge?

- Do I make obscene gestures at drivers who offend me?

The next step is to work on developing a different response to situations that ordinarily would get you fuming. Slow down, take a deep breath or three, and yield to the other driver. If not for yourself, then at least do it for the others close to you, for the people in the other car, and for your children who will be drivers themselves one day.

Your goal: Consciously work at being considerate of the people in your car and in the cars around you. That's how to combat road rage.

Of course, this process takes time. I'm working hard on it, but I still catch myself muttering under my breath or casting the evil eye at a particularly foolish driver. Overall, though, my attitude is getting better. For instance, I no longer do the tailgating trick to force a slow car in front of me to go faster. (It doesn't work, anyway.)

Yikes!

....

"My husband tailgates, changes lanes without looking over his shoulder to check the blind spot, and falls asleep at the wheel, saying, "I was NOT asleep," when we observe him over and over still doing it. (He totaled our car once after telling me this five times.)"

....

DRIVER'S ED-IQUETTE

While road rage is the most dramatic example of inconsiderate driving, there are other key behaviors that the thinking man should also keep in mind at all times:

Texting/Cell Phone Use

Just the other day my wife and I were waiting patiently at the first tee on the opening event of couples night at our golf club. Our friend Dan, whom we were playing with, was nowhere in sight and the starter was panicking. Suddenly Dan roared up in his car, jumped out, and hurried to the tee. It turns out he had been at a dead standstill for thirty minutes waiting for an accident to get cleared up. Cause: using a cell phone while driving.

Don't do it. It's dangerous, and in more and more states it's becoming illegal.

The Radio

It was surprising to see the radio as the third most frustrating behavior after aggressive behavior and misuse of cell phones. It's not just how loud men play the radio that is a problem. The radio, it turns out, is like a weapon. Men seem to use it as a means of keeping the other people in the car silent. Turn it up loud enough and no one can talk.

Disgusting Habits

The car is not a private bathroom. Yet too many of us (men and women, actually) treat it as a place where we can groom and care for our bodies with total freedom. We shave, floss, and comb our hair. But perhaps most revolting was the astonishing number of respondents who complain about men who pick their noses. You're not alone. Other people really can see you. And in some cases your grooming completely distracts you from driving and makes you a menace on the road. Do yourself and people in the other cars a favor and pick in private.

Use Your Blinkers

It's amazing how many people fail to use their blinkers properly. If that guy in the ten-year-old sedan had flashed his signal to let me know he was slowing down to turn, maybe I wouldn't have been up his tailpipe. (I know, it's still no excuse.)

Signaling all turns well ahead of time is the courteous—and safe—thing to do. The same goes for using your blinker to indicate when you're changing lanes on the highway. (In most states it's also required by law.)

"DON'T WORRY—I KNOW HOW TO GET THERE"

It's a funny thing about men and directions. Our survey results indicate that men really don't like to ask for directions and women really don't like getting lost. In fact, a man's reluctance to ask for directions was the third most common "annoying car behavior" cited by our women respondents, after aggressive driving and speeding.

What the "asking directions" issue is really about is letting go of your male ego and surrendering to the fact that it's not a loss of face to ask someone for help. In fact, the alternative may leave you looking pretty foolish. As a bonus, you'll find that if you trust in people, this trust will often be repaid in surprising ways.

To illustrate this point: One year, when my wife and I were on a trip to Italy, we wanted to drive the mountain pass leading to the famed Amalfi

Coast. The road up the pass is one of the world's truly great switchback roads, with magnificent views of Mount Vesuvius and the Italian coast around every turn.

The trouble was, after driving for quite some time we were hopelessly lost in Pagani and still at the base of the mountain. All we knew was that we must've missed a turn. Reluctantly, I pulled into a gas station to—you guessed it—ask for directions. The only saving grace for my male ego was the fact that my wife speaks Italian. She got out to ask directions. Whenever a good-looking woman approaches a cluster of Italian men and asks for help, a great discussion ensues. Finally, she came back to the car.

"Follow that man and his son," she said, pointing to two members of the group who were getting into a car. "They're going to lead us to the road we're looking for." We followed their car through a bewildering number of turns along the back roads of the town. Never in a hundred years would we have found the way on our own. Then the car suddenly pulled to the shoulder, and the man waved us on. "Turn right at the next intersection and just follow that road," he instructed.

I never got the chance to thank our guide and his son for going so far out of their way to help two Americans lost on the way to Amalfi. If they happen to read this: *Grazie mille.*

Poetic Justice

For years men have resisted the temptation to ask for directions, especially from their significant other who is sitting patiently in the shotgun seat in possession of the right information. Their egos just wouldn't let them go there. But guys love their gadgets and bought GPS units by the thousands. What is so remarkable is now they have this beguiling female with a British accent telling them when to make every turn. Go figure . . .

7

IN-PERSON COMMUNICATION

W hat we have here is a failure to communicate." The captain of the prison road gang in the movie *Cool Hand Luke* may have been a sadist, but he understood what it takes to make a relationship work. Look at any relationship that's in trouble, and it's a good bet the underlying problem can be traced to a *failure to communicate*.

These days, there are more ways to communicate than ever before: in person, over the telephone, by voice mail, e-mail, text, tweet, video chat—or even by writing someone a letter (for those of us who still get special enjoyment from sending and receiving snail mail).

But simply having these tools in your toolbox isn't enough. You have to know *what* tools to use *when*, and how to use them effectively. If you end up writing a long-winded e-mail, or prattling on and on over the phone until you bore the other person to tears, or becoming so tongue-tied when leaving a message on voice mail that your recipient has no idea what you're talking about, then all the technology in the world won't help you. The result will still be a "failure to communicate."

LA LA LAND

Half of all communication is listening. So being a good listener is critical to the success of your communication with your wife, significant other, family, friends, strangers, and work colleagues. Here's what one survey respondent had to say about men's listening skills:

"They nod their heads during conversation and when asked, have no idea what you are talking about. They don't take a vested interest in the conversation. They never ask questions when they have questions on the topic and instead drift off into la la land."

Repeatedly, female respondents commented on how men appeared to be listening but were not actually paying attention to the conversation. I can't help but see their frustration as a symptom of perspective. Why? Because I'm guilty. I admit it. I'll bet my wife wonders where I am or why I'm not focused on the conversation we're meant to be having. Worse yet, she's right. I'm probably not focused on what she's saying, I'm focused on whatever it was I was doing. For me, focusing on two things at once is difficult; to her, I'm not listening.

Almost half the survey comments about communicating had to do with the issue of men not listening. For the sake of peace, harmony, and a better relationship, there is a solution: Take a break from whatever you're focused on, look at the person, and focus just on her and what she is saying. Put the show on pause, and turn and listen to her instead of the TV. In general, focus on her when she's talking to you so you really hear what is being said. Try active listening, a technique in which you reflect or repeat back what is being said to you so the other person knows you are taking in what's being said. When you do this, she will really appreciate your effort:

"Not many men do it, but my partner listens to what I say and remembers it. He later comments on my ideas, thoughts, and feelings. He acts on my suggestions, no matter how casually I said it."

"Active listening. Especially when something happened in their partner's workplace or friendship that is causing anxiety and stress."

"Makes it safe to share and discuss concerns and/or issues."

Safe. That's what communication in a relationship needs to be. Out of that safety and sincerity grow trust, confidence, and a better, stronger relationship. Figure out how to focus on her. It's worth the effort for both of you and for your relationship.

The Importance of Listening

When you're trying to communicate, whether one on one or in a group setting, the skill of *listening to others* is just as important as your ability to express yourself. Besides paying close attention to what the other person is saying, *make it clear that you're listening carefully* by looking directly at the person who is speaking. Don't interrupt until that person is done making his or her point. Then respond by asking questions and offering observations based on what was said. Make a habit of listening effectively, and you'll find that your relationships will grow and deepen.

QUALITY OF VOICE

Your voice communicates a lot about how you are really feeling. If your words indicate genuine interest but your voice is a monotone, what's the message you are sending? You really don't mean what you are saying. Characteristics of quality of voice include the following:

- **Tone.** Anger, frustration, joy, concern. People react not only to your words but how they are said and the tone of your voice. When you were growing up, how often did you hear these words from your mother or father: "Don't you take that tone of voice with me." Oops.

- **Speed.** Speed kills. In conversation, speed makes comprehension difficult, so slow down. The people or person you are talking with needs a little time to process what you are saying, especially if it's a serious, important subject.

- **Speaking clearly.** Mumbling, grunting—not only are you hard to understand, it sounds like you're trying not to be understood. Instead of contributing to the conversation you sound as if you are trying to avoid it.

- **Accent.** People come from different nationalities, even different areas of the United States. If you have an accent that is different from the person or people with whom you are talking, it may make it more difficult for them to understand you. In that case, speed is doubly problematic. And speaking clearly becomes even more important for you to be understood.

LISTENING SKILLS

Good listeners honor the person they are with by the way they focus on that person.

Look them in the eye. Eye contact is a key part of any interaction.

Nod or say "Uh huh." Simple nonverbal cues can demonstrate that your focus is squarely on the person and not somewhere else.

Ask a question or repeat a point. Questions and comments show you are really a part of the conversation and are hearing what the other person has to say.

Avoid nervous habits. I have a bad habit of playing with things while I'm listening to someone: A paper clip gets bent into dozens of different shapes; I move the tableware around my place setting; I doodle pictures on my note pad. I shouldn't because each of these actions can distract the person who is talking to me. Even though I'm focused on the conversation, the message I'm sending to the other person is "I'm distracted."

Wait your turn. It is very annoying to be in midsentence and suddenly have the person you are talking to start talking right over you. A good listener waits for a natural break, that momentary pause before jumping in with a comment or question.

TOPICS

It seems that certain topics can dominate men's conversations. The problem is some of those topics really aren't particularly interesting to some people.

What's inappropriate? Sex talk.

Even worse are men who talk about their sex lives to just about anybody.

JOKES

Jokes can be a great conversational gambit, but be careful about the kind of jokes you tell. Off-color jokes may be funny when you're alone with your buddies, but they may be resented when in mixed company or in front of kids. If you can't be sure the joke will be well received, then it's better not to tell it.

"It Sucks."

I was asked to give a seminar to the staff of a large ski area including the ski and snowboard instructors. One issue the company wanted addressed was word choice. It turned out that some of the younger instructors were using a word that was actually costing the ski area business. Parents were writing comments indicating they weren't going to purchase any more family lessons because they were fed up with hearing it.

The word: *Sucks.*

That word really wasn't a swear word, but said repeatedly over an hour it became offensive to these parents. And that offensiveness was costing the company revenue. To the young instructors, the word was harmless—a normal part of their vocabulary—and shouldn't have elicited such a reaction. But it did. Even though a particular word you use may be totally innocent or acceptable to you, if the person you are speaking to is offended by it, then perhaps you need to find an alternative.

THE IMPORTANCE OF NONVERBAL CUES

When you're talking with someone face-to-face you give nonverbal cues that enhance what you're saying. Those cues can reinforce your words or belie them. When you're with another person, not only do the words you say matter, your image matters as well. You can roll your eyes and imply your disgust or frustration. You can purse your lips and suggest impatience or simmering anger. You can jiggle your foot or drum your fingers and communicate your nervousness. You can sit back, slouched, with your arms crossed and indicate your nonreceptiveness.

When you say one thing and your body says another, you aren't communicating effectively.

8

TELEPHONE COMMUNICATION

I love the telephone. I can think of no item in our daily lives that is more important, and none that is used more inappropriately by more people.

Bottom line: Our phones control us, we don't control our phones.

For some reason, as a society we have conferred on phone callers the unique right to interrupt us at any time, no matter what we're doing. Worse yet, the phone conversation has taken precedence over the in-person conversation. Want to talk to the person in the next office but he's busy with someone else? No way could you walk in and usurp his time for ten minutes. But call him on the phone and you can talk away, no problem.

This attitude of phone supremacy is just plain wrong—and we can change it, one person at a time. Here are two modest proposals for regaining mastery over the telephone:

1. When you're talking in person with someone and the phone rings, *don't answer it*. Let your answering machine or voice mail pick up the message.

2. If you feel you must answer the phone, *excuse yourself, answer, and tell the caller that you'll ring them back later. Then end the conversation.* Be sure to call back as soon as you can.

VOLUME CONTROL

People in the waiting areas of airports have heard it; train, bus, and plane passengers know it even better; and for office colleagues in adjoining cubicles, it's a painful fact of daily life.

I'm talking about telephone voice. You know the voice I mean—that booming, oblivious-to-the-world tone that everyone seems to adopt as soon as they answer a phone.

In fact, there's a good reason for our tendency to talk loudly on the phone. When communicating on the phone, we aren't being supplied with the visual clues we would normally have when talking with someone in person. As a result, we compensate by speaking in a louder voice. This habit may also have a historical component: When phones were first invented, people had to shout to be heard on the other end. Technology has solved that problem long ago, but people don't seem to have caught up with the reality. This is especially true if the other person's voice sounds somewhat distant. We automatically assume that we need to speak up to be heard as well.

Bottom line: Talk at your normal voice level, unless the person on the other end of the line asks you to speak louder. In most cases, an ordinary conversational tone works just fine.

A REVEALING QUESTION

Have you witnessed people using their cell phones in a rude or annoying manner recently? That's what a poll by AP/IPSOS asked Americans. The overwhelming response was "Yes." In fact 89 percent of Americans surveyed witnessed this rude behavior.

But when they asked Americans: "Have you used your cell phone in a loud or annoying manner?" a scant 8 percent admitted to doing it.

The danger with cell phones is that we don't see ourselves as being rude when we answer our phones while we're engaged in a conversation with someone. Even if it is perceived as being rude, we excuse the rudeness in ourselves because, well, it's my phone and the call may be important, and I'm paying for it so I'm going to respond to it when it rings.

But to the person we are talking with, we're rude.

The solution: Let the call go to voice mail. You can call back in a few minutes.

Better yet, be proactive. When you're with other people put your phone on vibrate or, heresy of heresies, turn it off. Be in command of your cell phone; don't let it control you.

ETIQUETTE IMPERATIVE
Who's More Important?

The person who is with you takes precedence over the person who is calling you on the phone.

Tips for Taking Control of Your Phone

- Be sure you have an answering machine, voice mail system, or messaging service—then let it do its work if the phone rings while you're in the middle of a conversation.

- If possible, turn off your phone's ringer whenever you're talking with someone in person—or at least set the phone on Vibrate/Silent Ring mode.

- If you're having a phone conversation and another call comes in on your call waiting, the same advice holds. Either ignore the incoming call and let your voice mail pick up, or break away briefly from your initial conversation with an apology, take the new caller's name and number, and call them back when your first call is done.

- When it comes to call waiting, the one absolute mistake is to end your conversation with your first phone mate in order to take the new call. This should never be done, short of an outright emergency or a highly unusual circumstance (like receiving a call from Australia or from your ninety-year-old great-grandmother). Your first conversation takes precedence; your attention belongs to that person and no one else.

THE CELL/SMARTPHONE

The cell phone is a decidedly mixed blessing. It's a wonderfully convenient way to communicate—but if a cell isn't used with consideration for the people around you, it can also make life miserable for everyone within earshot.

Voice Mail Is One Answer

Years ago when my wife and I went to the movies, we would tell the sitter where we would be. There was no number where we could be reached other than calling the theater itself in the case of dire emergency. Nowadays, during seminars I tell the audience that the proper course of action is to turn off their phones when sitting in a movie theater. As sure as the sun will rise tomorrow, someone will raise their hand to ask, "What if my babysitter needs to reach me? I need to leave the phone on in case there's a problem."

"You have two options," I answer. "Option one: Turn off the phone. Then, at the end of the movie, check for messages and call home if you need to. Option two: Put your phone on vibrate mode; then if it shimmies, get up, go out to the lobby, and answer it. Under *no* circumstances is it acceptable to leave it on ring mode or to answer the phone inside the theater. End of story." And refrain from texting and checking e-mail, too. The light from the screen is distracting, not to mention the alert noise when a new message comes in.

The "I'm Totally Clueless" Syndrome

Once, as I was waiting to board a plane, a woman standing in line spoke on her phone to a friend the entire time. On and on she went, about how she would be arriving soon and how they would be going out to dinner that night. Everybody in the jetway was forced to listen to the conversation—but she clearly had *no idea* she was subjecting us to her conversation.

The capper was when she began asking her friend where they should go to eat that night. They couldn't decide. Suddenly a hand reached out and tapped the lady on the shoulder. "I can suggest a good restaurant for you if it will help," the man belonging to the hand offered. She looked around, horrified—then quickly ended the conversation.

Everyone got a chuckle out of the situation—but unfortunately, not all examples of the "totally clueless syndrome" are as benign as this one. Instead of simply talking about where to eat, some people hold public discussions involving incredibly personal or confidential information. I've had people tell me they've overheard intimate details about peoples' love lives, a family member's life-threatening illness, or the vivid specifics of the most lurid gossip.

Bottom line: If you must make a call in a public place like an airport, restaurant, or theater, excuse yourself, go to the lobby, outside, or any other private place—then make the call where it won't disturb the people around you and where your private conversation will remain that way. And if you *must* make or receive a call while you're riding public transportation, keep it as short and low volume as possible.

Lodging Cell Phone Complaints

More and more public places are banning the use of cell phones. Commuters rebelled, and there are cell policies on commuter trains and buses. Public waiting rooms and doctor's offices request that phones and pagers be turned off.

If someone's cell phone use is disturbing you, make your complaint to management. It is then incumbent on management to enforce the rules.

In restaurants, if someone is talking on a cell phone and it's bothering the people at your table, talk to the waiter or maître d'. Have him or her address the issue with the offender. The same holds if you're at a movie theater, concert, or play: Talk to an usher or see the manager, and never try to approach the offender directly.

9

YOU ARE WHAT YOU WRITE—
WARTS AND ALL

Whenever you send a written communication, whether by regular mail or e-mail, your writing style will be on full view, warts and all. These mistakes reflect on you, so make a point of carefully reviewing everything you write, even informal notes.

THE HANDWRITTEN NOTE

Want to impress someone? Send them a note, in the mail, handwritten, on nice stationery. They'll be impressed. They'll remember you. And they'll think, "What a nice guy."

People often ask me, "Why should I write a note? Why not send an e-mail?" The answer is easy. If it's a choice between writing an e-mail or doing nothing, write the e-mail. But if the choice is whether to send a handwritten note or an e-mail, then the handwritten note may just be the ticket.

Think of it this way: With an e-mail, you type it, press Send, hope the e-mail makes it through any spam blockers, and then hope the recipient is interested enough by the subject line to actually read it. Once read, she closes it and hits the Delete button.

With the handwritten note, after it is written, you place it in an envelope, address it, put a stamp on it, and mail it. When the note arrives, the recipient invariably opens it. (Have you ever received a personal letter and not opened it?) Once read, it is placed on a tabletop, desk, or counter, or posted on a bulletin board or on your refrigerator with a magnet. It is seen again and again and each time it is seen, the recipient thinks of you.

Now, would you rather be deleted or remembered?

Send the note.

Thank-you Notes

- When you receive and open a gift without the giver being present, send a note.

- In fact, even if the giver is present and you thank her, send a note anyway. She'll really be impressed.

- When you stay at someone's house overnight, send a thank-you note.

- When you go to someone's house for dinner, send a thank-you note.

Congratulations

Send a note saying congratulations for graduating or on a promotion or new job, or when a new addition to the family has arrived or a special anniversary or birthday is being celebrated.

Bereavement

One of the hardest notes to send and one of the most appreciated notes to receive is the bereavement note. We all experience the loss of a loved one or close friend and when we do it is devastating. The notes of sympathy and remembrance are a catalyst to helping get through the pain of the loss. It seems like such a small thing from the perspective of the sender. But for the recipient those notes are a powerful comfort to help deal with the loss.

What to Say

It's easy. When writing a thank-you note, keep it short and sweet. Just three to five sentences is all you need.

Dear Kathy and Wendell,

What a great weekend! The party Saturday night couldn't have been better, and I enjoyed meeting all your new friends in Seattle. Hope we can get together again soon.

Thanks for making my visit such a pleasure.

Tom

Maximum time to write: ten minutes. Maximum benefit to you: incalculable.

THE STATIONERY DRAWER

One of the hardest parts of handwritten and personal correspondence is having the appropriate materials on hand when you need them. So, put the book down, and make tracks for your local stationery store. They'll help you select a set of stationery or you can order stationery in any one of a number of designs with your personal information printed on it. Items to include in your stationery drawer include the following:

NOTE CARDS. Either a flat correspondence card or a folded note with accompanying envelopes.

LETTER SHEETS. Smaller than the full 8½ x 11-inch paper, use it for longer personal letters and thank-you, congratulatory, or bereavement notes.

CALLING CARDS. Like a business card, a calling card provides essential contact information. In this case, it's your personal calling card. Include only the information that you want to give out, such as your name, home e-mail address, and phone number(s). You can also include items like a Facebook page or Twitter account address. For security, don't add your home address; you can always write it on the back of the card if you want someone to have that information.

E-MAIL HELL

E-mails are public documents. Period. The absolute bottom line: *If you can't post it on a bulletin board, then don't send it.*

Speed Kills

The speed we love about e-mail is also an insidious danger.

Here's the situation: You receive a nasty e-mail. Hopping mad, you decide to respond immediately. The words flow quickly, until finally you hit that last exclamation mark and, with great satisfaction, punch the Send button.

"That'll show him," you think to yourself. Five minutes later, feeling much calmer now, you reread your sent mail—and realize that it was way over the top. Unfortunately, there is no reliable way to retrieve it. Once you hit that Send button, your missile rockets out of your server and can never be recalled.

The problem with any immediate response is that it invariably will be much more about your anger than about solving the problem at hand. When penning any sort of message, *take your time.*

SIX TIPS FOR E-MAIL SUCCESS

Be Careful of the Subject Line

We spend so much time getting the body of an e-mail perfect, and then we quickly fill in the subject line and send it without realizing there's a misspelling or trigger word that will cause a spam blocker to prevent the recipient from receiving it. Take the same care with the subject line as you do with the e-mail itself.

And while you're at it, double check to whom the e-mail is going.

E-mail programs like to help you address e-mails. Start typing a name and the program instantly assumes you mean whoever you sent to last with that name is who you want to send to now. You start typing *S, a, r* and up pops <u>Sara@isp.com</u>. The only problem is you wanted to send it to <u>Sarah@email.com</u> but you don't notice the slipup. You hit Send and off goes the e-mail to the wrong person. Sometimes it doesn't matter, but in this case Sara is your new girlfriend, and Sarah is the girl you just dumped.

Proofread Grammar, Word Choice, Spelling

Typos, misspellings, grammatical errors—they all stand out and make you look sloppy.

Be Conscious of Your Tone

Tone of voice is not only something that is heard (see Chapter 7, In-Person Communication), it also is evident in your writing. You can hear what you sound like in your writing. Take your e-mail or note into an empty room and close the door. Then stand up and read what you have written out loud. You'll hear if you sound friendly or frustrated, calm or angry. If the tone isn't what you want, then you'll need to do some editing. If you're still not sure, have a friend or significant other read it out loud. I often take an e-mail I've composed and have a colleague read it just to make sure my tone won't be misinterpreted by the recipient.

Be Careful About Emoticons and Textspeak

Abbreviations and textspeak are great forms of shorthand. They can make communications like tweets or text messages easier to compose. But if the recipient can't decode them, then using them was useless.

b4 = before

lol = laughing out loud

cul8r = see you later

404 = I haven't a clue

swmbo = she who must be obeyed

Emoticons are used to make sure a recipient understands the tone you meant. A happy face ☺ or a sad face ☹ are most commonly used. The happy face at the end of a sentence says, "Just joking," in case you mistook the meaning; don't be offended because no offense was intended. With close friends, a happy face or other emoticon can be understood. But to someone you don't know well, it's better to rephrase what you said so it can't be misunderstood than to have to provide an emoticon to explain your meaning.

Formal vs. Friendly

With good friends and family, a friendly form of address is expected: Aunt Jane, Uncle Bill, Tom, Sally, Mom, Dad. But if you're writing to someone for the first time, then even in an e-mail, defer to the formal: title and last name: Mr. Smith, Ms. Jones, Dr. Dempsey.

Salutations

Salutations are the opening of an e-mail or letter: Dear Tom, Hello everybody, Cindy and John. You should start any e-mail, note, or letter with a salutation. In an e-mail stream, the first time you reply, you should include a salutation, but after that it's okay to drop it. Think of it as a conversation. Once you've acknowledged the person with their name, you don't need to keep repeating it every time you respond.

TEXTING: DANGER, DANGER, DANGER

Somehow we seem to think we are safe behind the electronic brick wall. We can text whatever we want, and we're safe. Dump a girlfriend? Easy, I'll just text her.

In-person communicating puts you squarely on the line, so it can be difficult to do at times. Texting seems like such an easy out. But the fact is, when difficult news needs to be delivered, doing it in person is the most respectful way. With a text, the hurt is doubled because you didn't even have the common decency to talk to the person face-to-face.

Save texting for factual, positive messages.

10

MEETING AND GREETING

Have you ever watched the TV game show *Wheel of Fortune?* One night I watched the usual celebration unfold at the end of the show, with the relatives rushing down to congratulate the lucky winner. This time, however, when Pat Sajak, the host, held his hand out to the winner to offer his congratulations, the winner chose that moment to abruptly turn away from Pat and kiss his wife. Pat stood there looking down at his empty hand, then looked up at the camera with a "What do I do now?" look on his face. Finally he shrugged his shoulders, retracted his hand, and waved to the audience.

In front of thousands of viewers, he gave a perfect demonstration of what happens when people don't do what's expected. When people know the appropriate manners for a given situation and use them, everything's great, and we all move on. When they don't, as in the Pat Sajak example, that's when confusion and hurt feelings can arise.

GREETING PEOPLE

There are four simple steps that help to make people think highly of you from the moment you first greet them. Here they are:

1. **STAND UP**. This is *always* the start of a good greeting, whether you're a man or a woman. By standing up, you engage the person you are greeting on an equal level—eye to eye. Remaining seated, on the other hand, sends the signal that you think you're more important than the other person and don't need to stand—not the message you want to convey at the start of an interaction, to say the least. If you're seated in a place where getting up is awkward, make a clear attempt to rise and apologize briefly as you greet the other person: "It's a pleasure to meet you, John. Please excuse me—it's a little cramped in here." If you are meeting someone who is in a wheelchair, bend down as you shake hands to get your eyes to a more even level with hers.

2. **SMILE AND MAKE EYE CONTACT**. A smile indicates warmth, openness, and a genuine interest in the person you are greeting. Making eye contact is also critical. Looking into a person's eyes shows that you are focused on and interested in that person. Doing the opposite, on the other hand—looking away as you greet someone—will make you appear aloof, disinterested, or rude.

3. **STATE YOUR NAME AND REPEAT THE OTHER PERSON'S NAME.** If you are the person who is initiating the greeting, your opening should be along these lines: "Hello, my name is Tom Meyers." If you are on the receiving end of the greeting, your response should be something like: "Hi Tom, I'm Jerry Smith. I'm pleased to meet you." If there are others in your group, you might add, "This is Cindy White and Jim Jones. Please join us. We were just talking about . . ." The key is to offer or acknowledge the spoken greeting, then invite the person joining the group into the conversation.

4. **SHAKE HANDS.** For more information on the all-important handshake, read on.

THE ALL-IMPORTANT HANDSHAKE

The handshake is a seminal moment in a greeting. The right handshake makes everything flow smoothly. The wrong handshake turns the focus to the error.

There are three types of handshakes—only one of which is acceptable:

- **WRONG: THE BONE CRUSHER HANDSHAKE**—Handshaking should not be a macho contest or a means of showing superiority, and it should *never* leave the other person in pain or discomfort.

- **WRONG: THE LIMP-WRIST HANDSHAKE**—This handshake feels like you're gripping a dead fish. It conveys neither warmth nor interest.

- **RIGHT: THE FIRM HANDSHAKE**—Grip firmly and warmly, without squeezing hard. Two or three pumps are all that's needed—so don't prolong the event by holding on longer than is necessary.

When it's obvious that someone has an injured right arm or is missing a right arm or hand, it's perfectly okay to extend your left hand for a shake.

Overly friendly handshakes should be reserved for very good friends. The "Bill Clinton" two-handed shake is a perfect example, or the "grab the person's arm with your left hand" shake. These are neither necessary nor expected. Just shake hands.

When It's Okay Not to Shake

Shaking hands is one of the most time-honored traditions we have. Not shaking clearly puts all the focus on why you chose not to shake rather than on building a relationship. One of the few times not shaking is not only appropriate but really important is when you have a cold or other communicable disease. People will appreciate your honesty if you say something like "Marge, please excuse me for not shaking, but I have a cold and don't want to give it to you. It's so nice to meet you." Or you might have just sneezed into your hand and not had a chance to get to a washroom.

ETIQUETTE IMPERATIVE

The Man-Woman Issue

Historically, men were not expected to shake hands with women. Today, as part of meeting and greeting, everyone is expected to shake hands with everybody.

MAKING INTRODUCTIONS

There you are, talking with someone cute and interesting you've just met at a cocktail party, when suddenly your great-aunt Winifred (I actually *had* a great-aunt Winifred) approaches. Instant panic: You want to make the introduction correctly, but several problems immediately rear their ugly heads: Who do you introduce to whom, how do you do it, and what exactly was Cute-and-interesting's name, again?

The Fist Bump

The fist bump, high fives, complicated handshake rituals, and hug/shake combinations—these are alternate means of greeting. When you're with friends and people you know who appreciate these forms of greeting, they are acceptable alternatives to the traditional handshake. However, if you don't know the person well, it's a business situation, or you simply aren't sure, default to the traditional handshake.

Hugs and Kisses

Traditionally, American men don't greet each other with a hug, at least not compared to many of their foreign counterparts. But that is changing. I see young men enjoying a friendly handshake-hug combo when they meet. As long as both of you are comfortable with the hug, it's okay. Go for it. But if you sense any hesitancy, do the other guy a favor and back off.

I recently visited Saudi Arabia where men greet each other with kisses on each cheek—right, left, right. While other cultures may appreciate a quick peck on the cheek, it's not found its way into the lexicon of American male greetings.

Who Do You Introduce to Whom?

Okay—let's take a deep breath and start at the beginning: Just talk to the more important person first.

CORRECT: "Mr. Important Person, I would like to introduce Mr. Other Person to you."

INCORRECT: "Mr. Other Person, I would like to introduce Mr. Important Person to you."

When Aunt Winifred approaches, first make the decision that she is the more important person in this encounter and say, "Aunt Winifred, how nice to see you!" (Kiss, kiss on the cheeks.) "Please, let me introduce Cute-and-interesting to you." (I'll deal with the problem of remembering her name in just a minute.) Next, turn to Cute-and-interesting and say, "Cute-and-interesting, this is Mrs. Post, my great-aunt Winifred. I'm so pleased to introduce you." Then turn back to Aunt Winnie and continue, "Aunt Winnie, we were talking about how cold the weather is. You just came up from Florida. How was it there?" And off you go . . .

So, Who's More Important?

When you make an introduction, the rule says first talk to the more important person:

A client or prospect is more important than your CEO.

An older person is generally more important than a younger person.

If it's a man and a woman and all else is relatively equal, make her the more important person.

Remembering Names (or Not)

We all forget names. I haven't met anyone who hasn't, at one time or another, been in the awkward situation of having to make an introduction when they were unable to remember one of the people's names.

So what do these folks do?

Usually nothing. That's right: nada. Zip. No introduction. Let them introduce themselves, goes the thinking, and get me out of the pickle I'm in.

Well, that might work in the short run. But I guarantee you that the people whom you failed to introduce will not appreciate you for making your problem into their problem. And I don't blame them one bit.

Okay, so what *should* you do?

Admit your problem and ask for help. Here's how it works. Let's say you've started the introduction. "Aunt Winifred! How nice to see you." (Kiss, kiss on the cheeks.) "Please, let me introduce . . ."

At this point, you stop and turn to Cute-and-interesting with an apologetic smile and say, "I am so embarrassed—I can't remember your name." Now, Cute-and-interesting could leave you hanging by not saying anything, but in all my forgetful years I've never seen this happen. Most likely, she'll reach out her hand to Aunt Winnie and say, "Hi, I'm Carmen Sanobel. It's so nice to meet you."

You say to Carmen (with heartfelt gratitude), "Thank you, Carmen" (thus imprinting her name on your forgetful brain). Then you turn to Aunt Winnie and continue, "Aunt Winnie, Carmen and I were talking about how cold the weather is. You just came up from Florida. How was it there?" And off you go. . . .

We've all been there, and we all know how it feels. The important thing is you were able to make the introduction. Carmen and Winnie are going to blow right past your small stumble because you did the important thing: You acknowledged them both and made it possible for them to start having a positive interaction—which is much more important than remembering Carmen's name.

On the other hand, you'd better make sure you imprint Carmen's name permanently on your memory from now on if you hope to see her in the future. It would be in *extremely* poor taste to have your great-aunt Evie (yes, I had a great-aunt Evie, too—*and* a great-aunt Florence) come over and have to ask Carmen for her name once again.

Some tips on remembering the names of people you meet:

Focus

I know it can be hard, especially if she's gorgeous and you're trying hard not to do or say something incredibly stupid. But no matter how difficult it may seem, you've got to forget her looks for one moment and focus instead on her face and on the words you are hearing.

"Tom, I'd like to introduce Gorgeous to you," your great-aunt Florence says.

What you don't do is mumble, "Nice to meet you." Instead, say with a clear voice, "Gorgeous, what a pleasure it is to meet you!" And as she replies, you repeat to yourself, "Gorgeous, Gorgeous, Gorgeous." Then make a point of saying her name out loud at various points during the conversation that follows. The goal is simple: *Imprint that name.*

Use Imaging

Another time-honored trick is to immediately picture some image or idea that you associate with the person's name. For example, you might think to yourself, "*Gorgeous—like in Drop Dead* Gorgeous, *the movie.*" This sort of association actually increases the amount of neural connections devoted to a particular memory, providing an automatic (and very effective) hint every time you find it necessary to recall your newfound friend's name.

"Nice to Meet You, Too."

....

It's happened to all of us: You approach a stranger at a dinner party, politely extend your hand, and say, "Hi, my name is Bill Owens."

The stranger extends his hand in turn and says, "Nice to meet you."

And that's all. No name.

This is one of the most vexing "meet and greet" problems I've come across. Bill is left hanging, thinking to himself, *"Hey, stranger. Have you got a name? What's the deal here?"* Meanwhile, the clueless stranger forges onward, repeating his transgression wherever he goes, assuming everybody knows his name. You could respond with something like, "I'm sorry, I missed your name. You are . . . ?"

Bottom line: Don't be like the stranger—unless you want to leave a poor first impression.

....

MR. AND MRS. OR JOHN AND MARY?

The real issue in the debate about using first names as opposed to a title like "Mr.," "Mrs.," or "Ms." is one of respect. For that reason, if you're with people who are older than you, or in a formal situation with people you don't know well, always start by using the more formal type of address. If the other person then offers you the opportunity to address him or her differently, politely thank them and proceed.

11

TIPPING 101

Ah, the dilemmas of tipping: Should you? If so, how much—and when? There was a time when you tipped to show your appreciation for good service. Nowadays restaurants in particular automatically figure in potential tips when deciding what to pay their workers. This allows the restaurant to pay lower wages—and turns tips into an absolute necessity for those workers. In these cases, the only way to show special appreciation is to tip *more* than the expected amount.

With other professions, such as furniture movers, the old concept still holds: They are getting paid a good salary to do their job, and any tip you give is considered an expression of thanks for outstanding service. The same goes for any business that posts a tip jar on the counter; in these cases a tip is not necessary, and whether you decide to leave one or not is totally up to you.

On the other hand, if you fail to tip when it's expected, you can be assured that the gesture will be perceived as being unfriendly—a message you probably don't want to send. Even in cases where the service is truly bad—for example, when your restaurant waiter is inattentive or rude—the wrong response is to leave a greatly reduced tip. This won't accomplish anything other than annoying your server. If there is a real problem with someone's service, leave a tip that's on the *low end of usual*—then make a point of taking up your complaint with that person's manager or supervisor.

APPROPRIATE TIPS FOR BUSINESS AND PROFESSIONAL SERVICES

Barbers

A tip of 15 to 20 percent is perfectly reasonable, but round up to the nearest dollar. The woman who cuts my hair charges twenty-five dollars, and I tip five dollars each time. It's easier, and she's worth every penny. If you are in a fancy salon in which different people provide hair washing, shaving, and so on, give a tip of one or two dollars to each service provider and a tip equal to 15 to 20 percent of the bill to the person who cuts your hair. When the owner cuts your hair, you don't need to leave a tip. But a gift at the holidays is considered a nice gesture.

Deliveries

A supermarket delivery person should receive around two dollars per delivery, more as the number of bags and flights of stairs increases.

Food deliverers usually get a tip equal to 10 percent of the bill because the delivery charge goes to the owner. The tip should be at least a dollar for a small pizza order, say five to ten dollars and at least three dollars if the order is larger or the delivery involves several flights of stairs.

Movers

The head mover gets twenty-five to fifty dollars and crew members should receive fifteen to thirty dollars each, depending on the amount of furniture moved. The tip may increase if they also packed your belongings.

Garage Attendants

Give a tip of a dollar to the parking lot attendant who brings you your car when you pick it up. If you keep your car in a garage, you may want to tip the attendants five dollars periodically to ensure prompt service; then offer a larger tip at the holidays.

Trash Collection

Hand out a tip of ten to fifteen dollars per crew member at the holidays. If your service is municipal, check to be sure there is no regulation preventing gifts to crew members before offering them.

Lawn Care

If there's one person who takes care of your place regularly, you can offer him or her a fifteen- to twenty-five-dollar tip at the end of the season.

Grocery Loaders

Tip a dollar if the loader helps you to your car with a normal number of bags and two to three dollars if you have a large number of bags.

Taxis

Generally, you should tip your driver approximately 15 percent of the cost of the fare—but never less than fifty cents. For a small fare like five dollars it is appropriate to tip 20 percent, or a dollar. In addition, rounding up the tip where appropriate will make life easier for you and a little more pleasant for the cabdriver. For instance, 15 percent of a twelve-dollar fare comes to $1.80; in this case, it makes sense to round the tip up to an even two dollars.

Private Cars and Limousines

If you get billed regularly by a car service, the best approach is to ask the company if a gratuity is included, in the fee. If not, ask the scheduler to add a 15-percent gratuity to the bill. This way everything is included, and you don't have to worry about fumbling for a tip when you arrive at your destination. If you are paying for the trip at the end of the ride, then tip the driver as you would for a taxi.

Sometimes a car service may be provided for you by a company or some other third party. In this case, offer the driver a five-dollar tip at the end of the ride. It's a nice gesture on your part. In Washington, D.C., I once had a car service at my disposal for an entire day. During my down-time between interviews, the driver took me to visit the Vietnam War Memorial, the Korean War Memorial, and several other sites around the Mall. I gave him an extra-large tip as a sign of my gratitude—even though someone else was paying the bill.

TIPPING AT RESTAURANTS

Coatroom Attendants

Tip the attendant a dollar per coat when you pick up your garments—and two dollars per coat if you've also checked parcels, umbrellas, or hats.

Washroom Attendants

You'll tend to see washroom attendants much more in Europe than in the United States, though there is a recent trend toward having washroom attendants at restaurants in larger U.S. cities. You should tip the attendant no less than fifty cents. Often the washroom will have a plate with some coins on it where you can leave your tip.

Waiters and Waitresses

Tipping waitstaff has changed from the traditional 15 percent. Today most people tip 20 percent, both out of generosity and because the math is easier. One important note: The tip is based on the cost of the meal *before* any taxes are added. If the waiter serves wine or any other drinks, then the cost of these beverages should be figured into the tip as well.

Waitstaff at a buffet-style restaurant should be left a 10-percent rather than 15-percent tip because they don't provide full service. Generally, bus staff are not tipped but receive a share of pooled tips.

Be careful to check the menu and your bill for any indication that a gratuity has been added to the bill, especially for groups of six or more people.

Maître d'

Usually you do not tip the restaurant maître d' or the host or hostess. The harsh truth is, tipping the maître d' is not really likely to get you a good table. On the other hand, if you go to a certain restaurant often, you may want to tip the maître d', host, or hostess ten to twenty dollars every once in a while to acknowledge their ongoing service and attention to your needs, if that's the case.

Wine Steward

If the restaurant has a wine steward who helps you select the wine and pours it for you, you should tip him or her the same percentage you will tip the waitstaff, usually 20 percent. I'm often asked, "What if I buy a four hundred–dollar bottle of wine? Doesn't it seem a little excessive to tip the wine steward eighty dollars?" My response: If you can handle buying a four hundred–dollar bottle of wine, then you can handle an eighty-dollar tip for the wine steward.

You can either tip the wine steward in cash when he pours the last of the wine or you can list his tip separately and add it to the bill at the end of the meal. Remember, if you do tip him separately deduct the price of the wine from the bill before figuring the tip for the waitstaff or you'll end up tipping twice on the wine.

Bartender

Generally, bartenders are tipped 20 percent of the bar bill. If you're at a restaurant and have drinks while you're waiting for your table, you should leave a 20-percent tip for the bartender before being shown to your table. Remember: If you do tip the bartender and the drinks are part of your total bill, mentally deduct the bar tab from the bill before figuring the tip.

Musicians

There are usually two kinds of musicians in restaurants—those who play in the background and musicians who go from table to table like traveling minstrels. Musicians who play in the background, such as piano players, will usually have a brandy snifter or some other container for tips. As with all tip jars, the decision to tip in this case is entirely up to you. Musicians who travel from table to table should be tipped a dollar or two when they visit your table plus a dollar for each request. Don't feel you have to wait for the musician to finish playing before tucking into your meal. You are there to enjoy your food, so feel free to eat while you're being serenaded.

Valet Parking

It's appropriate to tip the parking attendant one to three dollars when he or she brings you your car. In a large metropolitan area the tip may be as much as five dollars.

HOLIDAY TIPPING

Newspaper Delivery

You should give a tip of five to fifteen dollars at the holidays if your paper is delivered by a neighborhood youth. A somewhat larger tip is appropriate for adults who perform this job.

Household Help

A cleaning person or a regular babysitter should generally be offered a monetary gift equivalent to the cost of one service, plus a small gift. For a babysitter, the gift can be from the child(ren). Usually, you don't tip household help on a weekly basis. If you hire a person to do a onetime cleaning, then a 15-percent tip at the time of service is appropriate.

Similarly, don't forget dog walkers and plant waterers who also make your life easier throughout the year.

Residential Building Employees

Superintendents should typically be given a tip of around fifty dollars if they help with deliveries, fix things, or carry heavy items for you—ranging down to twenty dollars or less if these services are not provided.

Doorman

Give a holiday tip of thirty-five to fifty dollars for very helpful doormen, and less for those you don't interact with regularly.

Elevator Operator

A ten- to twenty-dollar tip at the holiday season is an appropriate thank-you for service provided throughout the year. If he or she does something special for you, tip at the time the service is given.

Doormen You Don't See

Your building may have several different doormen working at times when you don't see them, yet they provide a valuable service just by being there and being available. If your building has several doormen, check to see if a tip pool has been set up by the building to share tips for the doormen. You can always give the doormen who you see often a little something extra. The same is true for other residential building personnel.

TIPPING WHEN TRAVELING

I'm uncomfortable about tipping when I'm simply unsure of how much to leave. This issue comes up most often when I'm in countries other than the United States. I want to tip reasonably for the expectations of the country I'm visiting, but I simply don't know what those expectations are.

If you're traveling abroad, take the time to check online or read a good travel book on the region you're heading to—the good ones almost always include advice on tipping. The key is to pin down this information *before* you leave home, so you'll know what's customary once you reach the place you are visiting.

On a Ship

Cruise ships will generally provide a detailed gratuity schedule. Check with your cruise company or their Web site regarding this schedule before setting sail—then follow it.

At the Airport

Skycaps should be tipped two dollars for one bag and a dollar for each additional bag. Wheelchair pushers and cart drivers can be tipped five to ten dollars. Airline ground personnel and flight attendants are not tipped.

Motels and Hotels

Bellman: If he or she helps you with your baggage, tip a dollar per bag, but not less than two dollars in any case. Any additional service, such as bringing you a package, should be tipped two to three dollars each time.

Doorman: If he or she helps you with your baggage, again tip a dollar per bag but not less than two dollars in any case. If the doorman gets a cab for you, a tip of one to three dollars is appropriate, depending on the weather and how hard he or she had to work to get the cab.

Room Service: Tip 15 percent of the bill but never less than two dollars. Note that this is *in addition* to the hotel's fee for providing room service. The only exception to this is if the hotel has already added both a room service fee *and* a gratuity on the room service receipt.

Concierge: Generally, the concierge should be tipped five dollars for arranging your reservation, and so on. You can increase this amount if he or she has gone above and beyond the call of normal service. For example, tip 20 percent of the ticket price for hard-to-get theater tickets.

Housekeeping: The housekeeping staff is often ignored in the tipping department. Yet they perform a vital service, and saying "thank you" to them is as appropriate as it is for the concierge doorman or bellman. Depending on the hotel a tip of two to five dollars a day is appropriate. It's best to leave it each day in an envelope or with a note marked "Housekeeping—thank you" as staff may change from day to day.

12

WORKING OUT, OR, LOST IN YOUR OWN THOUGHTS

When men are working out, they tend to get lost in their own thoughts. More than once, I've waited for a circuit machine to free up, only to watch Mr. Oblivious finish with a set and just sit there, hogging the machine. He could easily have alternated sets with me—but he simply wasn't aware of what was happening around him or he just didn't care. In either case, he failed to realize the reality that in a public setting like a fitness center, you aren't alone. You're in a group setting that requires being aware at all times of how your actions affect others. Here are some of the most common fitness club flubs that men make:

LEAVING A POOL OF SWEAT

Mr. Buff is really pushing his physical limits on an exercise bike. Finally the session ends, and he steps off the bike, still totally focused on his effort, and walks away. Behind him, the handles glisten with his manly perspiration, and the seat has a small pool of sweat on it, waiting for the next lucky exerciser to climb on—maybe even that certain someone he's been trying to impress.

It's not that Mr. Buff refused to clean the machine on purpose—he just didn't think of it. His mind was far, far away, in an endorphin haze. Which brings us back to the central premise of fitness club etiquette: Be conscious of the people around you.

Imagine this scenario instead: When Mr. Buff steps off, he turns to the next person and says cheerfully, "Just a second—let me clean this off for you." A handy bottle of cleanser and a towel are nearby. He squirts the towel and then wipes the bike down. This is called being considerate. It's also a great way to make the right kind of impression on your fellow club member.

So Gross!

"They do not wipe down their machines and weights when they're done. So gross!"

Over and over again women spoke loudly and clearly about the failure of men to wipe down the equipment after using it. It takes just a minute. Fitness centers keep spray bottles and wipe-down rags nearby. A quick spray and wipe will do more to ingratiate you with your fellow fitness buffs than any other thing you can do at the gym.

By the way, it's not just women who are frustrated by this gross behavior. Twenty-nine percent of the respondents who brought up this issue were men and, by a wide margin, this was the biggest complaint about the fitness center in the 2011 Post Survey.

THE UNWANTED STARE

This one is a toughie. Those close-fitting sports bras and shorts don't always leave much to the imagination. And then there's all that uncovered skin—sometimes lots of it—not to mention the occasional tattoo.

Somehow I've always thought of a tattoo as an invitation to look: After all, why else is it there but to be noticed? The other day, for example, a woman on the yoga mat next to mine took off her jacket to reveal what looked like a large tattoo of Matisse's painting *Dance*, one of the great works of modern art, on her back. I had to consciously work at not staring at her. I would have loved to really study that tattoo, but I limited myself to a few discreet looks when her back was turned toward me.

The point is there's a difference between a look and a stare. Here's the distinction: When you look around you as you work out, your gaze falls naturally on another person but your focus is on what you're doing. When you stare, you focus on the object of your staring rather than on what you are doing.

The bottom line: Women know when you're staring at them, especially when you're staring at their breasts ("and I have normal-sized breasts," fumed one respondent). They don't like it.

Do you want to impress a woman? Then look, don't stare. And look in her eyes, not at her breasts. You'll impress her most by showing that you're a man who knows how to respect a woman, tattooed, large-breasted, or otherwise.

GRUNTING

"In through the nose, out through the mouth. Exhale!" Dana, my trainer, exhorts me. And then I realize I can hear myself. I wonder if other people are hearing me, too.

Now, there's a difference between an exhale—*whooooosh*—and a decibel shattering grunt. When your whoosh becomes a grunt you have crossed a line, and when you do, men and women are equally irritated. You don't have to grunt to exhale and when you do grunt, as one respondent put it so eloquently, "You're just showing off."

SURVEY SAYS
What Women Really Think About Macho Men

....

Here's what the women in our surveys had to say about men who are fitness club show-offs:

"Acts like an idiot trying to impress attractive women."

"Acts like Rambo when he's really one of the Three Stooges."

"Admires himself excessively in the surrounding mirrors."

"Flexes constantly."

"Grunts and groans excessively."

"Lifts more weight than he can handle."

"Shows off his form in a spandex suit when he's overweight."

....

THE "I'M MORE IMPORTANT THAN YOU ARE" SYNDROME

I was on a cruise ship recently where the line of jogging machines all face out the top deck windows, providing a fabulous view of the ocean as you work out. The sign-up system for these machines was pretty strict, I was told, for a good reason: It seems a woman had overstayed her time limit on one of the machines a while back, and the guy waiting took a swing at her when she didn't get off. Of course, she didn't help matters by refusing to get off the machine when her time was up. Both transgressors were guilty of the all-too-prevalent "I'm more important than you are" syndrome, which seems to be a hazard of working out.

The best way to deal with difficult people, and to avoid getting labeled as one yourself, is to respect the fitness center's rules:

- Follow the schedules for all machines: Start on time and end on time.

- Don't monopolize the machines. Don't use them as spare seats, and don't stand around them while talking with your buddies.

- If a conflict does arise, don't take it upon yourself to be the club policeman. Instead, point out the problem to staff, and let them take care of it.

- In the event that you're the culprit, admit your mistake forthrightly and make a conscious effort to change your habits.

HITTING ON WOMEN IN MIDWORKOUT

Do you ever read those relationship advice columns in men's magazines? They're full of guidance on how to meet women, and one of the places they often recommend is the fitness center. You've got to wonder if any of these writers has ever actually been to a fitness center. I admit the idea sounds great in theory: After all, it's a place where a lot of fit, attractive people are gathered to pursue a common interest. So what exactly is the appropriate pickup line when the woman you are interested in is sweating on the Stairmaster or straining to complete one last set of curls?

There isn't one.

Most women do not want some guy in their face, breaking their concentration while they're working out. What they want is to be left alone so they can do their routine.

The bottom line: Back off. Do your workout and let her finish hers. On your way out of the club, *after* you've showered and dressed (and are looking and smelling great), you can try striking up a conversation if the opportunity presents itself. At that point, *she* may even be interested in talking to *you*.

YOUR PERSONAL TRAINER IS A PERSON

My brother called me the other day. "Where were you?" he asked. "You weren't at your workout with Dana, and he was surprised because he said you always call or text him if you're going to miss an appointment."

I thought I had arranged with my wife that she would take my appointment and I would take hers, but we got our signals crossed and neither of us showed up. In five years of working with Dana, our personal trainer, I've heard over and over from him how frustrating it is to have an appointment not show up. He loses with the person who's skipped and he has a hole in his schedule someone else could have used, so from Dana's point of view he loses twice.

Personal trainers are like your best friend and confidant. So it's natural to assume that when you happen to see him at the gym you can stop by for a chat. Unfortunately for him and the client he is working with, your interruption takes away from the client's time with the trainer. While a quick "Hello" is totally acceptable, it's better to save longer conversations for breaks between clients.

Conversing with your trainer is a fun part of your workout (sometimes the only fun part), but be careful about gossiping. Sure, he's like a confidant, but don't say anything to him you wouldn't want posted on a bulletin board for anyone to read. Even if he's the most discreet person in the world, others working out nearby can overhear your conversation.

CLASS COURTESY

You can get a great workout from taking one of the many classes fitness centers offer members. Just be careful not to overdo it, and respect the other class participants as well.

Cleanliness Matters

Yoga class had started when "Jane" waltzed in and set up right next to me. Unfortunately, I almost had to leave the class. The smell was overwhelming. I felt awkward moving to another location so I had to bear it. Just because you're at a gym doesn't mean hygiene takes a backseat. Do your fellow fitness buffs a courtesy: Wash your clothes, wash your body, and use a deodorant.

Know Your Limitations

Don't try poses or push yourself beyond your body's limits. I've seen too many people exit a class and not be able to come back for weeks just because they pushed the limits and ended up straining a muscle. If you do want to try a new position or exercise, check in with the instructor ahead of time and get his or her help in making sure you can do so safely. If you're at a more advanced level than the class, it's respectful to ask if you can execute a more advanced move, say, a handstand instead of a headstand, before just going ahead and doing it.

Preexisting Conditions

Before you start a class, give the instructor a heads up about any injuries you may currently be dealing with. That way he knows the limitations you have and won't inadvertently push you beyond your current capabilities.

Call If You Can't Make a Class

Yoga and spinning classes are very popular at my fitness club, and there are often more people who want to attend them than there are open slots. These folks get very upset when someone blows off class without calling—with good reason. There are plenty of people on the waiting list who would have jumped at the chance to take that spot, even at six in the morning.

The bottom line: If you can't make a class you've signed up for, call the club well in advance and let them know you won't be there.

13

THE SPORTING LIFE: ON THE FIELD AND IN THE STANDS

I've seen athletics bring out the very best and the very worst in people. The satisfaction you feel after a hard-fought tennis match, the thrill of sinking a long putt, or the shared sense of triumph when a local team wins a championship are all examples of how sports can uplift us and bring us closer together. But when athletic enthusiasm veers over the line into unwelcome behavior—when a fan starts screaming at the referee, or a tennis player calls his opponent's close shot out when it's really in, or a golfer spends so much time on the course that he neglects his responsibilities at home—then sports can have the opposite effect: They start to interfere with our ability to get along with people around us.

In the heat of the "athletic moment," we sometimes forget that our behavior, both as participants and spectators, reflects on us in general. The fact is, *what you do and how you act during an athletic contest will influence other people's opinions of you.*

Athletics are competitive: The issues of winning, losing, and competing become emotionally charged—that's part of human nature. The problems start when we get so wrapped up in the moment that we forget our on-the-field behavior can eventually affect careers and relationships off the field.

I'm talking about more than merely yelling at refs. I'm talking about what happens when we become so consumed with the game that we ignore the people around us. (Sports widows everywhere are cheering right now—can you hear it?) I'm talking about what happens when we become so consumed with winning that we cheat in order to win. I'm talking about what happens when *competition* becomes more important than *people*.

IT'S OKAY TO WANT TO WIN

I've always been bothered by the phrase "It's not whether you win or lose that matters, it's how you play the game." This maxim implies that either you can care about winning or you can care about how you play the game, but you can't care about both.

To which I say, "Bull."

I admit it: I *care* about winning. I enjoy pocketing a bet from my weekly golf game. I like being on the winning side in a tough tennis match. I revel in the University of Vermont's hockey team's victories and suffer with them in defeat (lately I could do with a little less suffering and a little more reveling). But I also care about how the game is played. If I'm not "on" this particular week in golf and I play poorly, I may kick myself, or even sign up for a lesson to figure out what the heck has gone wrong. But I don't kick my ball to give it a better lie, or "forget" a couple of shots in the rough. I enjoy winning, *and* I care about how I play the game.

When it comes to striking a balance between winning and stretching the rules, amateur athletes have to be especially careful. Often winning seems to matter even more at the sandlot or in the backyard, where you're playing for "pride," than it does on the professional playing field.

"That's no touchdown—I touched you back by the sprinkler."

"You did not."

"Did too."

Look out—this could get nasty. You'd think the fate of the world rested on the outcome. What started out as a friendly game can quickly degenerate into an argument or worse, and suddenly a friendship is in ruins.

In this situation, "how you play the game" suddenly becomes very important. Bottom line: Being a good competitor matters. *People respect people who play by the rules.* Either you were touched or you weren't. Either the shot was in or it was out. Call the play fairly, accept the other person's opinion gracefully, and move on.

ETIQUETTE IMPERATIVE
Play by the Rules

No one likes a whiner or a cheat. On the other hand, I've often heard people talk admiringly about friends and competitors who play the game not only by the rules, but also by the spirit of the rules.

DO THE LITTLE THINGS THAT MATTER

Don't Be Late. For weekend athletes, time is precious. It's irritating for three men to be left standing on the first tee, wondering if number four is going to make it.

Don't Miss Appointments. There's nothing more frustrating than having three people show up to play doubles tennis at 6:00 A.M. If you can't make the scheduled match, it's your job to find a substitute.

Be a Responsible Borrower. Borrow my skis, borrow my surfboard, borrow my racquet. No problem. Break my skis, break my surfboard, break my racquet? Replace the borrowed piece of equipment with a new one of the same or comparable model. It's that simple.

"Yeah, but the one I borrowed was about to break," you say. "Why should I have to replace it with a new one?" Answer: When you borrow, you become responsible for what you borrow, warts and all. If you don't want the responsibility or if the equipment you want to borrow isn't in the best condition, don't borrow the stuff.

This also goes for your neighbor's tools or anything else you borrow. Once it's in your possession, you are the caretaker for the item. Lose it or break it? Then replace it or fix it like new. You'll stay good neighbors and good friends.

Leave Your Athletic Venue in Better Condition Than You Found It.
Before you leave the gym after your weekly hoops game, check the area
for all your belongings *and* for any garbage you or prior groups may have
left behind. When you walk onto the putting green, repair your ball
marks (the depression left when your ball first lands on the green) and
any others you happen to see. When you finish playing tennis on a clay
court, take a few minutes to sweep the court and clean off the lines for
the next players.

"Wait a minute," you say. "If the guys before us didn't clean up, why
should we?"

Whenever I talk to people about etiquette, they want to know why
they should be considerate, respectful, and honest when the people
around them aren't. The reasons are simple, really. First, we don't do
these things to get anything in return—we do them because we believe in
their inherent value. Second, nothing in this world is ever going to change
until someone starts the ball rolling. We arrive on time, we pick up after
ourselves, and we treat others with consideration, respect, and honesty
because it's the right thing to do. Lead by example—others will follow,
and we'll all be better off for it.

ETIQUETTE IMPERATIVE
Make It a Better Place

A candy wrapper on the ground, an empty bottle courtside—when you see a
piece of litter fouling your playing field, don't leave it for the next guy. Toss it in the
trash can.

CHEATIN' CHARLIE AND SANDBAGGER STAN— THE SCOURGE OF THE COURSE

There's no greater problem in sports than the guy who says to himself,
"Cheating is okay as long as I get away with it." You know who I mean:
Cheatin' Charlie always shaves a few strokes off his game—until it's club

championship time. Now every stroke counts, and players keep score for each other. Suddenly, Cheatin' Charlie, who's entered some pretty low scores, has to post a ninety-eight. Or maybe he'll quit halfway and post a DNF (Did Not Finish). He'll blame the playing conditions, his playing partners, or anything else he can think of—anything except the *real* cause of his problems: himself.

At the other end of the spectrum is Sandbagger Stan. This miscreant puts in scores higher than his handicap. The result: He can play significantly better than his handicap indicates. So when a net tournament is on the line he has a cheating advantage. Or when he's in a betting game, he increases the chances he'll walk away with the money. He'll also soon learn he has no friends and the tournament committee is onto him and changes his handicap or refuses him entry in the tournament. Nobody wants to play with Sandbagger Stan.

FRIENDSHIP VS. CHANGING THE FOURSOME

Paul recently posed the following question: "Every Thursday morning for the past four years we've played tennis with Sam. But lately Sam's become the weak link. We want to ask Andy to join us instead. How do we tell Sam we don't want him to play with us anymore without hurting his feelings?"

Poor Paul. He and his buddies know that their proposed switch will hurt Slumpin' Sam's feelings and will probably cost them their friendship with Sam off the court as well. Ditching a regular member of your sporting group for *any* reason is a very dicey thing to do. Ditching him because he isn't quite up to your caliber of play is simply not acceptable.

Before kicking him out, it's important to inform Sam of the group's decision. Maybe Sam is the cause of the breakup of another member's marriage. Now *that* would rise to the level of a legitimate reason for Sam to get kicked out of the group. The transgression had better be something pretty outrageous, though—because the decision to dump a playing partner, whatever the reason, is likely to cost a friendship.

A FRIENDLY WAGER

It happens all the time: a little action on the competition just to keep it more interesting.

In our regular foursome we joke that the winners of the two-dollar Nassau are really the losers because the winners buy the round of drinks after the match and that round costs more than the combined twelve-dollar winnings. It's the bragging rights that are important.

Just remember, once you make the bet, you're committed. Do not make a bet you can't cover. And if you lose, pay up, immediately.

The Usual Bet

Bob was in Las Vegas and wanted to play a round of golf. He was paired up with three local players. On the first tee teams were set up, and they agreed to play the usual. By the fourth hole Bob was in a sweat. Two of the three guys owned casinos and the third was a general manager. "Just how much is 'the usual'?" Bob kept thinking to himself. Finally, he got up the nerve to ask his partner. "We play a dollar on each side and two for the eighteen," his partner replied. It took Bob several more holes to calm down.

Know the conditions of your bet before you start your game.

THE GOLDEN RULE OF SPECTATING: KEEP IT POSITIVE

How do you know where to draw the line when rooting for your favorite team? Simple. You should feel free to shout as much encouragement for your team as you can possibly muster. But when your yelling shifts from being encouraging to derogatory—that's when you've stopped playing a supportive role as a spectator.

Any time you shout encouragement, the players on the field will feed off that energy. On the other hand, if your comments or cheering turn negative and you start berating or putting down the players, coaches, or referees, the effect will not only be counterproductive, but you'll also make people around you (who may or may not agree with you) feel uncomfortable.

Bottom line: Cheer all you want, but keep it positive.

Fanning the Flames

....

Unfortunately, there have been incidents where a fan of one team found himself surrounded by fans for the other team. Perhaps he pushed too far or maybe he didn't, but shouts turned to actions and in the end nobody won. If you're near fans of the other team, keep your cheering positive and let everyone enjoy the game.

....

REFEREES ARE PEOPLE TOO

I'd like to leave you with one final thought on spectating: *Leave the ref alone!*

One point that's often lost amid all the jeering at sports events is the fact that referees are people too. Basically, they want to make the right calls just as much as the players, coaches, and fans want them to. Referees are faced with a daunting task. A baseball umpire, for instance, might have to make 150 or more calls in a single game. If the baseball umpire makes three calls that could be considered questionable, that means he's still making 147 good calls. That's a 98-percent success rate. In most jobs, a 98-percent average would be admirable. For the umpire, however, those three questionable calls mean he's doomed to be on the receiving end of a torrent of abuse.

It gets even worse. You will also have perfectly sensible players, fans, and coaches who see a call one way while the ref sees it another. The ref is right, but that doesn't stop the fans from grousing about how they would have won if it hadn't been for him. They forget all about their team's missed plays, strikeouts, or blown shots and focus on the one call they claim "cost them the game." It's time for these complainers to grow up. The ref didn't cost them the game—their own team's players did.

14

PARENTS AND KIDS

According to Public Agenda, a research organization based in New York:

- Eighty-four percent of Americans agree that a major cause of disrespect in our society is the fact that "too many parents are failing to teach respect to their kids."

- Seventy-five percent of Americans want parents to teach their kids that "cursing is always wrong."

- Only 19 percent of adult Americans claim they "never curse."

These last two points highlight a major contradiction in American attitudes toward children's rude behavior. As adults, we're all part of the problem—and the potential solution. It doesn't matter whether you're a parent or not.

Children learn by mimicking adult behavior.

Let me repeat that: *Children learn by mimicking adult behavior.*

Example: You're standing in line at the grocery store with a buddy when a mom and her two kids get in line behind you. You're still hot under the collar from an incident that happened on the drive to the store, and you're not shy about letting your friend know your feelings.

"Crazy bastard," you snarl. "Can you believe how he cut me off? The bleep almost hit me! I should have chased him down and taught him a bleeping lesson."

You are, in a word, oblivious. Meanwhile, the young children standing a few feet away from you have imprinted the following images in their memories:

1. *A grown man swearing*—which must mean that it's okay to swear, at least if you're really mad.

2. *A grown man threatening revenge*—which must mean that it's okay to do violence to another person if you think there's enough justification.

The bottom line: You don't have to have kids of your own to have an impact on children.

When it comes to teaching kids to be more respectful and less rude, there is no silver-bullet solution. It's a process that involves all of us and that will take time. We all need to recognize that how we act will be reflected in the behavior and attitudes of tomorrow's adults. If every adult starts making a conscious decision to model considerate, respectful behavior in his or her daily life, kids will start reflecting that behavior. The sooner we do this, the sooner our children's positive behavior will be reinforced.

ETIQUETTE IMPERATIVE
Children Mirror the Behavior of Adults

Be extra careful around children. You're already influencing children every time you're around them by the way you act, speak, and carry yourself.

Before Arrival

....

It lasts nine months, usually, and for most of them you're going to know something is changing. While that something isn't you, it will affect your life significantly.

She's going through a lot as her body grows and nurtures the baby. She'll need your support now more than ever. So be there with her. Learn what is happening.

Make an extra effort to lighten her load. Cooking, shopping, cleaning, doing the laundry are chores she might usually handle, but now she's going to need your help. Rather than waiting for her to ask, step up to the plate and do it, not just once but consistently.

Be a little more loving. A back rub, a foot massage while you're watching television. Hold her hand (women love this). Show her you are her partner and you are there for her. It's a special time, and you can do a lot to make it a *positive* special time.

....

SO NOW YOU'RE A DAD!

On June 12, 1979, Anna, my oldest child, was born. At the time, I had no idea how much my life would change as a result. My wife and I had been married for six years, and now . . . all of a sudden, there were three of us.

Our living situation had altered drastically—but old habits die hard. June is strawberry-picking time in Vermont, and about ten days after our daughter was born, I went berry picking. There happened to be a crop of luscious berries that day, bright red, juicy—the height of perfection. I got carried away and came home with a couple of flats full of berries.

In previous years, this sort of hunter-gatherer action on my part would have been hailed as a feat of initiative. Now, however, with a two-week-old baby in residence, the only reaction my wife had was, "What on earth am I going to do with those strawberries? I don't have time to make jam or put them up."

I learned two lessons that day: First, things had definitely changed, and I had to start recognizing that fact. Second, putting up strawberries and making jam is a lot of work.

SURVEY SAYS

What Women Really Think About Men Helping with the Kids

On the impressive side:

"My husband plays with my children in a way I just can't do. I think it's important for my daughters to have a father figure in their lives who gets down on the floor and plays silly roughhousing games."

"Helps with bedtime routine."

"Teach good things to their children, stay active and engaged in their children's lives, growth, and development."

"Help with children's homework."

"Sees the needs of our son and steps up without being asked to do so."

On the annoying side:

"Men don't pitch in with the kids unless they're asked to."

"They resent having to watch the kids while you go out."

"They opt out of the discipline process, leaving the woman to be the only parent who disciplines the children."

"They don't think to initiate bedtime routines for kids."

"Men ignore the kids if they're otherwise occupied."

How do you see yourself in these comments?

SHARING THE RESPONSIBILITY

Being the male parent is not simply a matter of taking a larger role in chores around the house in order to take pressure off your mate so she can focus on raising the baby. Being a male parent also means being a part of the child care—and not just in the first few weeks. It means being an equal partner in the care of your children for the next eighteen years, and then some. Child care takes a couple of different forms:

- **SHARING THE LOAD.** This sometimes involves serious sacrifice. For instance, on any given Sunday afternoon, just as Tom Brady throws a Hail Mary pass to put the game into overtime, the phone rings. My daughter is on the line: "Can you pick me up now?" My wife's making dinner, so I have no choice.

- **BEING THE DISCIPLINARIAN.** Dads can't always be fun. Discipline is part of parenting, and for it to work, both partners have to participate. The mom can't always be the heavy. She will resent you no end if you're always the parent who consoles the child. Be willing to be a parent who enforces the law, and support your spouse in her choices when she's the enforcer.

- **GOING TO THEIR EVENTS.** I've heard more primary school holiday concerts than I care to remember. Each one was important to my daughters, and it was also important that both of their parents were there to share in their performance. Whether your child is the star or a member of the chorus, you make time to attend, you applaud thunderously, and you congratulate her as though it were opening night on Broadway.

- **TALKING WITH YOUR KIDS.** Take the time to listen to your children. They have wonderful thoughts and an ever-fresh perspective, and talking with them will help bring those thoughts out. When I was a young parent, I could always tell the kids whose parents listened to them. If I was driving them home after a visit, they were the kids who would talk your ear off, even though you were a relatively unfamiliar adult. Those conversations were always a joy, especially compared to driving a kid home whose vocabulary consisted of grunted, monosyllabic responses to my questions.

Time passes so quickly. Before you know it, those little toddlers will be off living on their own. So make the effort to share in the raising of your kids. In the process of raising them, you'll build a stronger relationship with your spouse and give your kids the best possible opportunity to grow up happy and successful.

Do as I Say, Not as I Do

The statistics reveal how much we Americans buy into this maxim: Seventy-five percent of adult Americans want to teach children not to swear. But at the same time, 81 percent of us acknowledge swearing ourselves at least some of the time.

In other words, we admit that we're modeling this behavior even though we want and expect different behavior from our kids.

Learning doesn't work that way. I discovered this when my older daughter was in grade school. She had a teacher whom I firmly believed was the perfect example of what's wrong with the "guaranteed job" policies in public education—and one day I voiced my displeasure about her *in front of my daughter*. I remember it so clearly. A short while later, during a discussion about a problem my daughter was having with her teacher, I heard my daughter spout my words back at me. The lightbulb immediately went off in my head: How could I possibly expect her to follow my admonition to "respect her teacher" *when I was teaching her to disrespect that same person?*

Kids do not understand "Do as I say, not as I do." They do understand "Do as I do."

....

COACHING YOUR OWN KIDS

A good friend of mine coaches his son's lacrosse team. When I learned this, I couldn't help but think: Here's a formula for disaster. But it happens every day and dads can do it successfully.

Be Impartial

The key is to look at your child as a team member and not as your son or daughter. You've taken on the job so you have one very difficult task. This can be tough when it's your child who is sitting on the bench. At the start of the season, talk with your child. Explain that you love him or her but you also have to be the coach for the team and that means no favoritism. It's important not only for both your sakes but for the effect your impartiality will have on the other players and their parents as well.

Coach Positively

Yelling, berating, and/or sarcasm don't work as motivators, especially for children. Children want to learn; they want to improve. And they do it best when their teacher, parent, or coach instructs them in a positive, constructive way.

SPECTATING AT YOUR KIDS' SPORTS EVENTS

We are so proud of our kids. We want them to do well. We want their team to be the best. And sometimes we get carried away: We see a call that seems to be unfair, and we scream at the ref. We see the coach call our son or daughter out of the game, and we scream at the coach. We see a teammate make a bonehead play, and we scream at the teammate. We see our own son or daughter miss a play they've made hundreds of times in the backyard, and we scream at him or her.

All this screaming doesn't work. The referee isn't going to change his call; the coach isn't about to suddenly see things your way and send your kid back in; the teammate isn't going to magically turn into an all-star candidate. And your son or daughter is now likely to be more focused on your incessant, embarrassing screaming than on his or her own play.

Youth leagues now have spectator standards, and they're serious about enforcing them. They'll even require parents to watch a video and sign a statement promising that they'll adhere to the league's standards of spectator behavior. They're serious: one infraction and the offending parent is placed on probation. A second infraction and they're banned from attending future events.

THE SOCCER DAD

Chatter. Whispering. Complaining to each other. Parents do it all the time with other parents on their kids' youth teams. Frankly, it drives the coaches and the league organizers crazy. The parents band together and then approach the coach. "Strength in numbers," they think to themselves. If you believe this is a good idea, I have a bridge in Brooklyn I'd like to talk to you about.

You're a parent, you're in the stands, and you should be supportive not only of your kids, but of the coaches and the program as well. If others start jabbering, try to stop them or at least refuse to be part of their grousing.

PART TWO

SOCIAL LIFE

15

THE BEST AND THE WORST IN SOCIAL LIFE

When it comes to considerate behavior, most people tend to be a bit more on their toes when they're socializing—which is a good thing, because the standards are higher in these situations than when you are relaxing in your living room. And as our survey found, women both notice and *care about* how men behave in their social lives.

When we asked our respondents which male social behaviors bothered them the most, acting in a superior manner—bragging, putting others down, interrupting, dominating, ignoring, criticizing—topped the list. The other chief complaints involved men who behave boorishly—swear, pass gas, drink to excess—and who fail to treat women with the common courtesies like opening a car door, holding a coat, or walking on her correct side.

Fortunately, our respondents also had very good things to say about men who excelled in some of these same areas: When we asked them to name things they liked about male behavior, by far the most frequently cited items were mastery of manners, being caring and affectionate, pitching in, and being appreciative and proud of their significant others despite their possible shortcomings.

THE MOST IMPRESSIVE THING MEN DO: USE GOOD MANNERS

Manners absolutely, positively make the difference in social life.

The key to social success is not to think of "social etiquette" as a series of traps you can stumble into but as a terrific opportunity to do things right, thus pleasing and impressing those you're with. The most telltale result from the 2011 Post Social Life Survey was that although poor manners was fifth on the list of negative behaviors, good manners were cited most often as behaviors that are appreciated. Women notice and appreciate the chivalrous man more than any other. When respondents were asked to describe what men specifically "do well" in social life, they mentioned things like the following:

- Holding coats, elevators, doors, and chairs for women

- Carrying packages and heavy items

- Being careful to make introductions

- Walking beside a woman rather than ahead of her

- Offering an arm for support and affection

- Saying "please" and "thank you"

- Simply "being polite," "being a gentleman," or "being chivalrous"

These gestures are the mark of a man who is aware and respectful of the people around him. Men who got the best grades on manners from their significant others don't just do one of these things right—they instinctively do all of them right most of the time. It's the cumulative effect of good manners that creates a lasting positive impression.

ETIQUETTE IMPERATIVE
Doing It Every Day Makes the Difference

Just holding a door once probably won't make a difference in how she sees you. Do it consistently over time and she will notice and appreciate you and your thoughtfulness.

THE IDEAL ESCORT: APPRECIATIVE AND ATTENTIVE

Disrespect and inconsideration have a flip side: being appreciative and attentive. According to survey respondents, men who show appreciation and genuine interest on a consistent basis are the cream of the crop. They stand up for the other guy and refuse to engage in deprecating conversations. They defend the honor of their significant other, date, or friend. They remain calm and collected in the face of adversity. They selflessly offer to assist others in need. In essence they follow the golden rule: Do unto others as you would have them do unto you.

ETIQUETTE IMPERATIVE
Taking the High Road

- "Show kindness and humility."

- "Take the high road."

- "Refuse to engage with other men who are being juvenile."

- "Refuse to fight or argue."

- "Show respect to women."

- "Show respect for different viewpoints and ways of being."

If you really want to be an appreciative and attentive escort, good communication skills are vital. At least 90 percent of the positive comments about men in this regard involved issues of communication, such as including others in conversation, listening to what others have to say, and complimenting others on their thoughts, appearance, or actions. When it comes to making other people feel appreciated, these facets of human interaction make all the difference in the world.

DRESSING SMART, SMELLING FRESH, LOOKING GOOD

Ever notice a couple out for dinner or at the movies? The woman is dressed nicely—perhaps she's wearing some tailored pants or neat jeans or a skirt with a sweater or a jacket; and if you got close enough to notice any scent you would probably catch a light whiff of perfume. Then there's the guy with her—turned out in wrinkled jeans or scruffy pants, a T-shirt (probably with some inane slogan on it) or a work shirt that still carries the evidence of that afternoon's chores; his hair's a little unkempt and his scent is one you'd rather not notice. They've got to be hitched—because if they weren't she'd drop him like a hot potato.

In the Post social life surveys, poor appearance ranked number three among things that disturb women about men. Once again, the good news is that you can score big points by addressing this issue head on. According to our respondents, women particularly like it when men do the following:

- Make a little effort to "put on the dog"

- Know how to dress properly for the occasion

- Dress appropriately but not ostentatiously

- Dress up for a special occasion without complaining about it

- Take pride in their appearance without having to be reminded or prodded about it

We are not talking fancy here: We're talking about voluntarily dressing and grooming yourself in a way that is appropriate for the occasion. Perhaps the most important comment in the above list was the one about men who "take pride in their appearance." I like this respondent's philosophy. She understands that when you look in the mirror, you need to appreciate how you look. When you're able to appreciate your appearance, that's when others are going to say, "He looks sharp." And they'll admire you for it.

Combine good grooming with good manners (which, as I've said, is nothing more than treating people with consideration, respect, and honesty) and a willingness to communicate by listening to, focusing on, and complimenting your companion and others—and you have a foolproof recipe for social success.

ACTING IN A SUPERIOR WAY—MEN AT THEIR WORST

When men engage in behaviors like bragging, interrupting, ignoring, or acting condescendingly, the women who are with them view them as inconsiderate oafs. If you act in a superior manner and you're with a live-in significant other or a spouse, the result is likely to be a very cold shoulder later in the evening or, worse, a bitter fight. If you're out with a date, there may not be another—and you may find your reputation starting to precede you as well.

FOUL LANGUAGE FOUL

Over the past several years I've been telling my business etiquette seminar participants that swearing is becoming a bigger and bigger issue in the workplace and companies are starting to institute "no swearing" policies. That trend is equally noticeable in social life. Swearing was the second most mentioned inappropriate behavior right behind acting superior. The message was clear: There's too much profanity, and it is not appreciated.

"I wish more men would refrain from using bad language around women, children, and also people they don't know. Not all men use bad language, and I feel that it makes one come off as boorish and less intelligent."

The Joke's on You

I am not a joke teller, but I know some guys who are just awesome at telling jokes. In the right company, in the right situation, a good joke is a great addition to a conversation.

Unfortunately, men have a propensity for telling the wrong joke to the wrong audience and causing embarrassment if not downright disgust. Repeatedly respondents complained that joke tellers spoke before they thought. Before you tell a joke, stop and think for a minute: "Will everybody who hears this joke appreciate it?" If there's even the slightest chance it could be offensive, then silence is golden.

16

DATING—JUST YOU AND HER

When a man is out on a date (and this is equally true whether you're with your wife or on a first date), doing the little things with confidence goes a long way toward setting the right mood. When you're doing all the little things to make your companion feel special, your date can focus completely on having a great time rather than on the things you aren't doing.

JUST YOU AND HER

Sometimes I think my eyes have a mind all their own. There I am with my wife, my attention is on her, we're talking and having a great time. And then it happens. Maybe She walks by, or sits at the next table, or comes around a corner, or steps out of a cab as we're walking down the street. I must have pretty good peripheral vision because I usually notice Her. I try hard not to let my head snap around, but the distraction gets the better of me. If it is a really impressive distraction, I may even take a quick breath, the kind that makes a little sound. The surveys are abundantly clear on this point: When you're out on a date or with your significant other, noticing other women is a real mood killer.

Most women recognize that men are going to look at other women.

The real key is not to let that stunning woman walking by interfere with your focus on the woman you're with. What you say and do throughout the evening will let her know she is perfect in your eyes. So say and do those things often.

- "You look great!"
- "Every other guy at the party is going to be jealous of me tonight."
- Buy her some flowers when it's not an event.
- Call her up and invite her out on a date with you. Give her specifics: restaurant, play, movie, concert.
- Cook dinner tonight.
- Hold her hand.

REMEMBERING AND CELEBRATING SPECIAL OCCASIONS

Men really are from Mars and women from Venus. More than once I've heard my daughters and their girlfriends talk about celebrating their "three-month anniversary." *"Huh? What three months?"* I'd think to myself. Of course . . . that's how long they'd been dating their most recent boyfriend.

But when it comes to the important special occasions, men are stepping up to the plate even if they don't realize it. In the 2011 Post Survey approximately 60 percent of the men agreed that they were good about remembering their significant other's birthday or their anniversary or Valentine's Day. However, when women were asked if their significant other was good about remembering these special days, approximately 75 percent said they did. Way to go, guys!

THE IMPORTANCE OF FLOWERS

Every time we go to the supermarket, my wife buys flowers. We live in Vermont, where it's pretty monotone all winter. Late fall and early spring—make that mud season—are colorless, too. Putting flowers in a glass vase on the dining room table is her way of fighting the seasons when things don't grow.

If I bring my wife flowers, I make her day. The problem is, I hardly ever bring her flowers. And hardly ever isn't nearly enough.

So I finally got smart. For her birthday I realized I had the perfect gift staring me in the face. I went to the local florist shop, which is her favorite place, and gave a standing order that once a month she can come in and pick flowers that are just right for her and for that time of the year. They charge the flowers to my credit card. Twelve times a year she gets her favorite birthday present from me. That's better than just once.

If you really want to express love and affection, nothing beats roses. They're great for that special someone in your life. She could be your wife or fiancée, a girlfriend or just a friend. Roses are especially appropriate when you are celebrating an anniversary or an extra-special event. But you don't need to wait for a major occasion—you can simply make one up.

"These are for you. I realized it's been one month since our first date."

Roses for My Bride

When my wife and I got married, I arranged to have a florist deliver a bouquet of six roses to my wife five days before our wedding. Four days before the wedding he delivered five roses. You get the idea. On the morning of the wedding he delivered a single rose. It's amazing the effect one rose can have. Be creative.

OPENING DOORS

All things being equal, as I approach a door with my wife, I'll step forward ever so slightly, open the door, and hold it for her to enter before me. If I'm carrying a parcel or if for some reason she is clearly there ahead of me and starts opening the door herself, I don't make a scene by rushing forward and pushing her aside so I can open the door for her. Instead, I accept the effort she is making and say, "Thank you." Other times, when she arrives at a door first and starts opening it, if I can I'll reach behind her and take hold of the edge of the door, discreetly taking over the task of opening it and then holding it for her so she can enter first.

Opening a door when entering and exiting a building is a considerate thing to do. The 2011 Post Survey found that 78 percent of respondents expect that a man should be prepared to open a building door all the time. Yet the same expectation does not hold true for car doors. While 39 percent said men should always get the car door, 56 percent indicated this is an action that needs to be performed only some of the time. That some of the time would be when on a date.

THE REVOLVING DOOR DILEMMA

Confusion reigns over this issue because it involves conflicting rules: the rule that a woman should go through a door ahead of her companion versus the rule that a man should enter a revolving door first because the door is heavy. Whenever confusion exists, the solution lies in communication. The real problems arise when you act indecisively. So be prepared to make a quick decision as you're approaching the door: "This door looks hard to move, so I'll be the gentleman and offer to go through first" or "Look, the door is already moving, meaning it'll be easy to push—so I'll be the gentleman and suggest that she go first."

Once you've made your split-second decision, immediately communicate your intentions to your companion. "Please go ahead." Or "Here, let me go first and get it moving for you." Be confident, and act confidently. The situation will resolve itself, and you'll come through looking good.

HELPING HER WITH HER COAT

This one's easy.

Do it. And then take both coats to the coat check and get the claim ticket. When you leave, make sure you leave a tip of a dollar per coat in the tip jar.

WALKING TOGETHER

The convention here is that the man always walks on the outside (the side closest to the street). Most of the time this works very well. Imagine, for example, that you are walking down the street with your date, holding hands, and it comes time to cross to the other side of the street. As you get to the other side, you realize that you're now on the inside. You can make a smooth move behind her as you step up onto the sidewalk and now you're still on the correct side.

The one exception to this rule is when you have reason to feel that walking on the inside of your companion is appropriate for safety's sake. In this case, by all means do it.

ETIQUETTE IMPERATIVE
When You're Waiting . . .

When you're waiting to be seated at a restaurant or for the valet to bring your car, take a moment to smile at her. Tell her how great she looks. Take this moment and enjoy it with her.

STANDING

I've always believed that one of the most awkward moments at a dinner table occurs when the woman next to you gets up to go to the bathroom. Do you stand?

The 2011 Post Survey is clear on this point: Women want and expect you to stand up, at least when you are out on the town. So if this is impossible—for example, if you're in a booth—don't worry about it. But all things being equal, stand whenever your companion does.

Whenever you arrive at a table for a nonbusiness meal, offer to hold a chair for the woman seated next to you on your right. If the man next to the woman on your left fails to do his job, you can offer to hold her chair as well. You may even get an appreciative smile and a "Thanks." Likewise, when rising from the table at the end of the meal—provided you can do it without causing a scene—you should help move your dinner companion's chair away from the table by grasping the back and gently pulling as she starts to push it back in order to stand up. It's a nice gesture on your part.

The one exception: When you're at a business function, do not hold a chair for anyone, male or female, unless there is a physical need, or if you think a woman of an older generation would expect it. If you are unsure, ask, "Would you like me to get your chair for you?" Problem solved.

WHO PAYS?

When it comes to paying the bill at a restaurant, it's simple: The person who does the inviting pays for the meal. This rule works equally well in the business world and in your social life.

If you do the inviting, expect to pay and do so without hesitation. If the woman does the inviting and you're uncomfortable having her pay for the meal, talk to her about this when she first extends the invitation. You might offer to "go dutch," for instance. It's a nice gesture, and if she refuses then you know she was really serious about inviting you and picking up the tab.

If she invites you to an event, on the other hand, that leaves an opening for you to make a counter-invitation of your own, such as: "That would be great. I would love to go with you. May I take you to dinner before the concert?"

TO FLIRT OR NOT TO FLIRT?

Let's cut straight to the heart of the matter: Forget the word *flirting*. The underlying issue is *your intent*. Specifically, I'm talking about whether or not you've struck up a conversation with another person *with the intent of starting a personal, one-on-one, evolving, and <u>potentially</u>* intimate relationship with that person.

If the answer to this is yes, then you're flirting—and you are immediately subject to flirting etiquette, as follows:

- As long as *neither person is married or in a serious relationship*, then this kind of behavior is perfectly acceptable as long as it is done in an appropriate setting.

- If this sort of behavior is undertaken by two people, one or both of whom is married or in a serious relationship, then it's unacceptable.

In the course of my normal social life, I banter, joke, converse, enjoy innuendo, and indulge in fun, engaging, relaxed, and sometimes even racy conversations. By my definition, however, I am not flirting with the women with whom I am talking. Why? Because I have no intention of taking things any further than that particular conversation. In fact—and this is very important—nothing I do or say in these conversations involves anything I'd be embarrassed to tell my wife about later or to have her hear at the time.

When You and Your Partner Disagree

What happens when you assume that your racy conversation with that female aerobics instructor at the health club wine-and-cheese social was perfectly okay but your wife or significant other, watching from across the room, perceives your banter as a blatant come-on? Answer: You've got a problem that needs resolving—and quickly.

Simply put, if one person in a serious relationship feels that the other partner's behavior is straying over the line, that opinion must be respected—and the "flirtatious" partner needs to start revising his or her behavior in a way that you *both* find acceptable. It's an issue worth talking about openly with your partner: Remember, strong, trusting relationships are built on honest communication, which entails clearly saying what you both mean and listening carefully to what is really being said by the other person—rather than only hearing what you want to hear.

17

ON THE TOWN

People like to watch sitcoms like *Two and a Half Men*, *The Big Bang Theory*, and *The Office* because they hit home. By providing a humorous look at the conundrums that arise among friends, family, and workmates, these shows allow real people to enjoy the spectacle of fictional characters facing (and working through) difficult and embarrassing situations without any real people getting hurt.

And therein lies the problem for us mortals. Unlike TV's fake "friends," when personal misunderstandings or disagreements crop up in our own social circles, people can feel hurt or embarrassed or disappointed or left out, and our situations don't get resolved in twenty-four minutes.

In our surveys, respondents consistently identified several key "group issues" that are most likely to give rise to discord: dividing expenses equitably, especially at a restaurant, and inconsiderate behavior by individual group members—what I call "small grossnesses," but that can have a big effect on group morale.

SHARING EXPENSES

It's great to be the host, or the guy with the car, or the guy with the boat. But sometimes it can be lonely—especially when it's time to open the wallet and pay for the drinks and munchies, the gas, or any other expense.

When it's not your house or your boat or your car, think about the other guy. Offer to chip in and buy a tank of gas or pick up supplies for the next poker game. He may never ask, but you can be sure he'll appreciate your contribution.

BAR ETIQUETTE

Bars are great places to hang out with your friends or meet new people. The problem is that slips and mistakes, which can be compounded by alcohol, can turn a fun evening into a disaster.

Before you go out, assess the situation you are going to be in. Understand clearly if it is a purely social evening or if it relates to business. I know one man who enjoys going to bars, but he simply never lets loose if he's out with people from work. He knows he's always making an impression on people even when it is completely outside the confines of the office.

Buying a Drink

What a nice gesture. Maybe it's even an opening gambit in getting to know someone new. But remember that offering to buy a drink is an offer without a quid pro quo. And when you make the offer, she may take you up in spades. Instead of a pleasant midpriced drink or a glass of wine, she may order a cosmopolitan. Once you've made the offer, you're on the hook.

If you do offer to buy a drink, make sure that she sees the bartender make it and that it is delivered to her without any chance of its being "doctored." This is for her safety and yours as well.

"Loose Lips Sink Ships"

Be very careful about the content of your conversation in a bar. You and your fellow workers or friends may think your conversation is private, but in fact you have no idea how easily the people at the next booth or bar stool may hear what you are saying. Keep work topics at work and private conversations for private places.

Buying Rounds

If a group of people goes out, rather than buying individual drinks, each member of the group may buy a round, in a "this one's on me" spirit. Just be sure that one of the rounds is on you. Nothing annoys people as much as those who don't carry their share of the load.

Alcohol

Going out to a bar with some friends, relaxing, shaking off the stress of a hard day's work—it is all lots of fun as long as it doesn't get out of hand. Be wary of the dangers of the effects of alcohol, especially as they can make you a little more combative and argumentative without your even realizing it. Guard against getting into a fight—physical or verbal.

ETIQUETTE IMPERATIVE
The Friend Who Has One Too Many

Friends don't let friends drive under the influence of alcohol. Be responsible and take away the keys, call your buddy a cab, or sacrifice your couch for the night.

THE ETIQUETTE OF SPLITTING THE BILL

Consider this dilemma: Donald and his wife, Mary, frequently go out to eat with two other couples. Don and Mary don't drink, while their fellow diners all enjoy a glass or two of fine wine over dinner. What's more, Don has recently changed his dietary habits, and nowadays he often orders a simple soup and salad while everyone else goes for an appetizer and a main course.

When it comes time to pay up, their ritual has been that each couple pulls out a credit card and the bill is split into three equal parts. Lately, however, Don can't help noticing that he and Mary are invariably subsidizing a fair portion of their friends' meals.

"I'm getting tired of this," Don says to himself. "Our share of last night's bill was eighty dollars, but Mary and I only ordered fifty dollars' worth of food." Don also values his friendships, so he suffers in silence, the pressure inside him slowly increasing, building toward the day when he finally blows. And that does promise to be an awkward moment.

If you are one of the Dons of this world, there are two things you can do to remedy the situation. In either case, talk with one or both of the other males before you head out to the restaurant. Don could say, "I'm looking forward to tonight, but I could use your advice. Mary and I have stopped drinking and, well, I've cut back on the amount I'm eating, too—trying to do something about this gut. Anyway, with us ordering less, how would you feel . . .

Option #1: ". . . if I ask the waiter or waitress for a separate bill for Mary and me?"

Option #2: ". . . if Mary and I contribute our part of the tab in cash, and you guys split the rest of the bill? That makes it easy for everyone, and maybe a little more even all around."

Either approach accomplishes two goals: Don lets Tom and Bob know what he is going to do so no one will be surprised at the restaurant, and he offers a reasonable solution rather than simply complaining about the problem. Result: Don ends up paying what's fair, and no one is embarrassed or confused. Problem solved.

There's another point to make here: Bob and Tom and their companions were a bit clueless, at best, about the awkward situation they were putting Don and Mary in. (At worst, they were taking advantage of Don and Mary, which is really bad news—and could be a sign for Don that it's time to seek out some new friends.) The best solution would have been if someone else in the group had recognized the problem and suggested that the "even split" policy was no longer fair to Don and Mary. For example, Tom might have said to the waiter, "Do us a favor, please. Put fifty dollars on this [Don's] card, and split the rest between the other two cards. Thank you."

Tom should do this discreetly, without making a big deal about it. In return, Don should offer his and Mary's appreciation for Tom's understanding. Then everyone can sit back and enjoy a wonderful friendship.

SMALL GROSSNESSES

Fingers vs. Forks with Shared Plates of Food

"Let's share an appetizer sampler," you suggest. Your friends all agree enthusiastically, and soon a large plate of fried calamari, melon and prosciutto, or other delicious hors d'oeuvres arrives. You start to reach for a piece of calamari when, directly to your right, Jared suddenly turns away from the table and sneezes. He quickly wipes off his nose and hands, and then grabs a calamari with his fingers. You suddenly lose your appetite—for good reason. While it was nice of Jared to turn his head and avoid spraying the food, he still made two glaring mistakes. First, he failed to excuse himself from the table to wash his hands after sneezing. Second, he used his hands to take items from a communal plate.

Then you realize, "I was about to take a calamari with my fingers, too—and nobody saw me licking my fingers a few minutes ago."

You resolve from now on to start using a serving utensil whenever you're eating from a shared plate.

Coughs, Sneezes, and Other Sudden Gusts

You can't stop a sneeze. But you can make an effort to avoid spreading your germs over the table. When I feel a sneeze coming on, I'll turn away and cover my mouth with my napkin. If the sneeze comes on fast, I'll at least bring my hands up to my face and look down into my lap as I sneeze. Then I'll excuse myself and head for the restroom to wash up. (If the sneeze turns into a sneezing fit, I'll go directly to the restroom to let it play itself out.)

What about putting your face into the crook of your elbow when you sneeze? That's what they now teach in primary school to stop the spread of germs. That may work when wearing everyday or Saturday clothes, but it's not a good technique when wearing a cashmere sweater, dress shirt, or nice jacket, which could be ruined.

The same goes for coughing: Put your hands to your face, turn away if possible or at least look down, then excuse yourself and head to the restroom to wash up.

Burps and passing gas are largely a matter of self-control—so practice it. You can do it. I know you can. Simply excuse yourself and retire to the restroom. No explanations are necessary.

If a burp escapes by mistake, the proper response is to say, "Excuse me. It happened before I could stop it." Once in a long while, you can get away with this. Make it a habit, though, and you may find yourself eating alone.

If gas passes unexpectedly, this can be a bit more embarrassing. If the episode is silent and unnoticeable, count yourself lucky. If not, be prepared to apologize to your immediate neighbors: "Oh, my—I'm so embarrassed. Please excuse me." Even though you may be red-faced for a moment, you'll save your companions from the embarrassment of others thinking one of them is the culprit.

18

THE GOOD GUEST

Dinner out at a friend's home is a staple in most people's social lives. It's a time to relax, enjoy company you know you like, and take part in what is usually a great meal.

THE INVITATION

How enjoyable the evening is for you and for your hosts is largely dependent on you, and it begins as soon as the invitation is extended.

The RSVP

The message light on our phone was blinking. "Peter, we'd like to invite you guys over for dinner Saturday night. Can you make it?"

So it starts. Now my wife and I have an obligation to fulfill, one that is far too often neglected and is incredibly annoying to hosts: to answer the invitation.

Repeatedly in both business and social forums I hear about inconsiderate invitees who don't respond. A host can't begin preparations unless he knows how many people are attending. This is especially true for a larger party or event but matters even if you and your significant other (or date) are the only guests. Unfortunately, when you don't respond, the only way the hostess can be sure of your answer is to call you. "Peter, I'm following up on the invitation I left on your voice mail last Monday. Do you think you can make it for dinner on Saturday?" Not really pleasant for her and somewhat embarrassing for you. You can avoid the awkward call by answering the invitation right away.

If you don't know if you can attend, at least call and let the hostess know you got the invitation and when you will get back to her with an answer.

Should You Bring Something?

The time to find out if you can bring anything to contribute to the dinner is at the time of the invitation. "Jane, we'd enjoy coming to dinner. Can we bring anything—a salad or dessert maybe?" Jane may accept your offer or she may simply indicate that your presence is all that's requested. If she doesn't ask you to bring anything, it means she's got the meal planned, so defer to her wishes and don't make your triple-layer chocolate cake for dessert. It simply creates an awkward situation for Jane, who may now feel she must serve your dessert instead of the one she prepared.

Changing a "No" to "Yes" or Vice Versa

Unless you're really ill or there's another serious conflict, don't change a "Yes" to a "No." Changing a "No" to a "Yes" is okay but only if it won't upset hosts' plans. In that case you'll need to explain the circumstances and ask if it is still okay for you to come. If not, don't be offended. Typically, if the party is a buffet or cocktail party, it'll probably be okay; but a dinner party for six where the host has invited another couple in your place, probably not.

Recently I traveled to Boston to do a seminar. We were invited to a friend's for dinner back in Vermont. Whether I could make it back in time depended upon when the event ended and on the traffic leaving town.

My wife accepted for herself and gave my regrets, explaining the situation. Our hosts graciously kept my invitation open, just asking that I call them on my way home after I'd left the Boston traffic behind. I did just that, and the timing worked so that I could join the party—a memorable meal and a delightful evening. The underlying message here is to let your hosts make the call.

Bringing a Guest

You open the door to greet your guest, Joe. Only it's not just Joe at the front door, it's Joe plus his best friend and wife who are visiting him for the weekend.

"Look who arrived unexpectedly. I knew you'd be excited to see them so I asked them to come, too."

You have two choices. Slam the door in Joe's face or welcome the two uninvited guests and quickly adjust the seating at your table. I even know of hosts who intentionally cook more food than needed for a party on the assumption that someone will bring an uninvited guest. Nice but not necessary.

If you are magnanimous and let the uninvited guests in, it's important to contact Joe the next day and let him know the dilemma he put you in. "Joe, I was surprised to see Sally and Jim with you. We really had to scramble to have enough food for everyone. If that happens again, could you please call ahead of time and let me know so we can talk about it. I'd really appreciate it. Is that okay with you?"

Bottom line: Don't bring uninvited people to a party or event. The most polite way to handle the situation is to let the host know ahead of time that you won't be able to attend because you have houseguests or can't find a sitter. The host can then either accept your regret graciously or take it upon himself to extend the invitation to the houseguest(s) or kids.

ETIQUETTE IMPERATIVE
When the Invitation for Us Comes to Me

Since I got married, I've learned one lesson: Never make plans without checking with my wife first. "Zach, that sounds great, but let me check first and make sure we don't have other plans. I'll call you back later." Now, I'm on the hook. I've got to check with my wife and then one of us has to get back to Zach ASAP. Keeping him hanging without an answer is inconsiderate to say the least.

AT THE PARTY

The day of the dinner has arrived and you've spent it out in your garden. Sure, they're good friends and all, but they still deserve the respect that cleaning up and dressing for the occasion demonstrate. A quick shower and shave and a set of fresh clothes, and you're almost good to go.

THE HOSTESS GIFT

If your hosts don't take you up on your offer to bring something and you still feel you *must*, I suggest bringing some flowers—which are always welcome and enhance the evening without affecting the menu. Bring them in a container or offer to arrange them yourself so you don't add one more task on the host's already full list of things to do.

An alternative to flowers is a bottle of wine. If you bring wine, explain that the wine is for your hosts' enjoyment anytime they like and you aren't expecting them to serve it that evening. "Here's a little something for your cellar."

Another option that is always appreciated is a box of chocolates.

What Is Fashionably Late?

Socially late is a euphemism that people think excuses lateness. It doesn't. That said, arriving up to fifteen minutes late probably isn't going to be a problem. But when you start going over fifteen minutes to half an hour or more, you've stepped over the bounds of what is reasonable. If you're going to be more than fifteen minutes late, call your host and let him know to start without you. Your host should not be delaying his dinner schedule for you because you couldn't get to the party on time.

Your Smartphone

This one's simple. Turn your phone to vibrate/silent ring mode or better yet, turn it off. Leave it in your pocket for the duration. If you must answer it, move outside or to a private area where taking the call won't disturb the other guests. And while at the dinner table leave it out of sight and don't look at it to read a text or use it to take or make a call. Period.

Top Six Ways to Be a Good Guest

1. R.S.V.P. Tell your host whether you can attend, and do so immediately.

2. Be on time: Do not arrive early or more than fifteen minutes late.

3. Be a willing participant: Partake of whatever the host offers—party games, the mushroom soufflé, chatting with a new acquaintance.

4. Offer to help when you can.

5. Don't overindulge: whether it is the pâté or the cabernet.

6. Thank the host twice: on your way out the door and with a phone call or a written note the next day.

Be Considerate

When in someone else's home, take extra care to show respect in the way you treat that person's home and belongings.

- Wipe your feet when you enter the home.

- Respect house customs, such as when you're asked to leave your shoes at the door. (The host of a "no shoes" home should provide slippers for guests to use.)

- Use a coaster for your drink.

- Don't be a snoop.

- Own up to any problem you cause like breaking a glass, spilling wine, or clogging a toilet.

- Smoke outside if you must at all.

- Don't put your feet up on the furniture, and use couches and chairs for what they are meant to be used: sitting in.

- Offer to help pass hors d'oeuvres, mix drinks, or clear the table.

Leave with the Others

All good things must come to an end. Take notice of when other guests are leaving and head out at around the same time.

THANK YOU

As you prepare to leave make sure you find your hosts and thank them for inviting you and for the wonderful evening. Then, the next day, call and express your thanks again and/or write them a note. We have a good friend who writes us every time she comes to dinner. Those notes are a pleasure to receive, and we are sure to invite her back time and again.

Reciprocate

The party's over; the thank yous have been made. What's next? It's your turn. Part of socializing is going to other people's homes to enjoy an evening together. But there is a social obligation to reciprocate and invite your friends over to your house as well. Chapter 19 takes a look at how to have a date or friends come to your home.

19

ENTERTAINING AT HOME

Whether you're happily married, or a single guy keeping house for yourself, there will invariably come a time when you want to invite guests over. The first prerequisite for entertaining at home is to have a *clean, orderly* residence where your guests will feel comfortable. This is true even if you're only planning to catch a ball game on television with your frat brothers. It's even more true if you are arranging an intimate, home-cooked meal for a special someone.

Here's the scenario: You ran into Monica two days ago at the coffee shop. You'd met her a few weeks earlier when she came along with your friend Lisa to an Ultimate Frisbee game at the local park. You talk Ultimate Frisbee for a few minutes and laugh about the great time you all had. Then you pop the question: "Hey, Monica, I love to cook. Would you let me make dinner for you sometime? Maybe we could go see a movie afterward. I could even ask Jim and Lisa to join us and make it a foursome. Or not—it's up to you."

You're on a roll here. By offering to cook dinner for Monica, you're really showing off your best side. Then you ice the cake by suggesting that you invite another couple along, ensuring that she'll feel safe and comfortable coming over to your place for a date.

"Sounds great! I had a good time with Lisa—it'll be fun to see her again," Monica says with enthusiasm.

It's not until you're well on your way home that reality sets in. *"What was I thinking?"* you ask yourself. *"My place is a pigsty, I don't really know how to cook, and I'd better make darn sure that Jim and Lisa can make it!"*

CLEANING UP—THE RIGHT WAY

First impressions are very hard to change—and this is Monica's first impression of how you live your life. Fail to clean up properly, and she'll have that introductory "you're a messy guy" image burned in her mind forever.

Keeping your residence neat and clean isn't only about making a good first impression, of course. Maintaining a clean, livable home is a way of showing respect and consideration for anyone who stops in, from your next-door neighbor to your longtime girlfriend. If you've moved in with and/or married your longtime girlfriend, then doing your share of the housecleaning—without complaining or needing to be prompted—is one of the best ways you can show consideration for her. It also affords the two of you the freedom to welcome others to your home at any time.

Unfortunately, as I mentioned in Chapter 2, when it comes to cleaning up, we men have a bad habit of thinking that it's okay to do a half-baked job. Think of it as a business project—one that will automatically enhance the short-term value of your real estate.

Start by tackling the kitchen: Scrub the counters, clean the stove surface, sweep and mop the floor thoroughly, and clean out your refrigerator.

Next, move on to your living room area: Put away any papers, clothes, or sports equipment you have scattered around, then dust all surfaces, vacuum and/or sweep the floor, and straighten the furniture and plump up the couch pillows.

Now move on to the bedroom: Make the bed (you might even want to change the sheets), put the dirty clothes in the hamper, and straighten up the bureau and shelf surfaces. Even if you're not going to end up there at the end of your date, she may catch a glimpse of it on the way to the bathroom.

Last, but far from least, comes the bathroom. For this all-important room, refer back to our discussion in Chapter 4. I'll simply remind you that in addition to cleaning your bathroom, you should also remember to make sure you have a full roll of toilet paper on hand, along with a fresh set of hand towels and a fresh bar of soap in the soap dish. A spray deodorizer will also be a welcome touch.

Take Care of Your Pets

If you have a cat, make sure the litter is fresh and doesn't smell; if you have a dog, walk it before your guests arrive.

THE K.I.S.S. SCHOOL OF HOME ENTERTAINING

If you're less than adept in the kitchen, then the value of the advice to "Keep It Simple, Stupid" will be self-evident: By doing a few things and doing them well, you'll spare yourself headaches and leave yourself free to concentrate on having a good time with your guests. The simplest plan of all is to order great takeout or prepared foods from a deli or specialty store. But this advice also works if you're a gourmet cook, or if you're sharing the entertaining duties with your roommate, wife, or significant other. Trying to plan an overelaborate event is a surefire recipe for stress and conflict.

THE K.I.S.S. MEAL PLAN

Plan a menu that allows you to do as much of the food preparation ahead of time as possible so you're free to focus on your guests. Before deciding on your menu, be sure to find out if any of your guests is vegetarian or has other dietary restrictions, including any food allergies.

Vegetarians, Vegans, Macrobiotics . . .

You're going to have a variety of people at your table. While it isn't necessary to prepare different meals for different people, it is helpful to plan your meal to ensure that all your guests have plenty to eat. Even if you're a meat eater, a couple of different vegetables, a starch, and a salad will cover most situations. Friends who are on special diets may offer to bring their own food. If they do, agree and make space for them to prepare it and plate it.

While you don't have to cater to each person's particular dietary needs, you can try to plan a menu that takes those needs at least somewhat into account. For instance, Joan is a vegetarian and you're grilling steak. Make sure the menu includes a couple of vegetables and a starch like baked potatoes; that way Joan can enjoy a full meal and not feel like she's being singled out.

K.I.S.S. Appetizers

For hors d'oeuvres, serve two or three. Possibilities include cheese and some crackers, olives, chips and salsa (medium or mild so you don't scorch a sensitive palate), or fresh veggies and some ranch dressing for a dip. Kick it up a notch with prosciutto wrapped around bite-size pieces of cantaloupe, smoked salmon on small squares of pumpernickel bread sprinkled with lemon and capers, bacon-wrapped scallops, or popcorn shrimp (available premade at your grocer or Costco). The pièce de résistance: caviar on toast points with lemon.

K.I.S.S. Main Course

Choose a menu that uses a few simple ingredients—preferably in a dish involving a minimum of pots and serving plates.

Don't be shy about asking friends and family for ideas—everyone has at least one favorite party recipe. I like to grill food, so one of my favorites is rack of lamb. I marinate it with olive oil, minced garlic, fresh rosemary, salt, and pepper, then grill it to medium rare. I'll serve asparagus that I also grill after lightly coating it with olive oil. Sliced tomatoes from the garden add color to the plate. Add a side salad and I'm set to go!

K.I.S.S. Dessert

For dessert: cookies and ice cream, a pie from a local bakery, fresh fruit. There are great pastry and bakery shops out there in most communities, so you're sure to find something delicious while sparing yourself a ton of work.

LAST-MINUTE DETAILS

Use the hour before your guests are due to arrive to go over all the final touches: Make sure the table is set properly, the white wine or beer is chilled, the ice bucket is filled, the lemons and limes are sliced, the music is ready to play, and the serving area is organized so that when the food is ready, it gets to the table before it gets cold. Lighted candles are always a fine mood setter. Now, take a moment to put your feet up, have a look around, and take in the warm, inviting scene. At the very least, your guests will be completely bowled over by the care and time you've put in on their behalf. Most likely, you'll all have a memorable time. And Monica? Let's just say that, at the very least, your relationship will be getting off on the right foot!

The Perfect Host

Fifteen years before Emily Post wrote her first etiquette book, when she was still famous mainly as the bestselling author of romantic fiction, she defined the perfect host in one of her novels. The book, *The Title Market*, is set in Rome in the early 1900s. The scene describes an Italian princess hosting a party at her home:

Throughout the evening there was the simplest sort of buffet supper: teas, bouillon—a claret cup, perhaps, and chocolate, little cakes, and sandwiches; never more. But the princess was one of those hostesses whose personality thoroughly pervades a house; a type which is becoming rare with every change in our modern civilization, and without which people might as well congregate in a hotel parlor. Each guest at the Palazzo Sansevero carried away the impression that not only had he been welcome himself, but that his presence had added materially to the enjoyment of others.

....

THE GOOD HOST

A clean home, great food, pleasant music—these elements all contribute to a great evening. But the one element that really makes or breaks a gathering at your home is you—the host. It's your job to make sure everyone feels welcome and to be attentive to each and every guest:

- Greet guests when they arrive.

- Circulate among your guests, introduce strangers, and stay long enough to get a conversation started.

- Keep an eye on your guests and offer to refill drinks as needed.

- Make sure the appetizer plates are replenished as needed.

- Balance the need to cook with taking care of your guests, so keep your menu simple.

- Thank each guest for coming when they prepare to depart.

If you accomplish these things, the occasion is guaranteed to be a success for everyone involved.

ETIQUETTE IMPERATIVE
When a Guest Asks: "May I Bring Something?"

....

Unless it's a potluck affair or the meal is a group effort, a thoughtful host never asks his guests to bring anything. And unless it's a formal occasion, a thoughtful guest always volunteers to bring something.

....

Double Dipping

You're hosting a party, and you decide to make a special effort by serving a big platter of shrimp along with a bowl of cocktail sauce. Everyone gathers around for the feast. The procedure is simple: Grab a shrimp, dip it in the sauce, and enjoy.

Then it happens: Across from you Dainty Debbie takes a bite and then, to your horror, dips the uneaten portion back into the sauce bowl so she can have a little sauce with her next bite. Several other guests look at you and silently speculate: *"What's he going to do?"*

"Let me see if I can freshen up this plate," you say to no one in particular. You pick up the platter and go to the kitchen, where you spoon out the area where Debbie double dipped or, better yet, replace the sauce with some you still have left because you were smart enough to buy extra.

P.S. Don't even think about giving the sauce a quick stir. While this may seem to be the easy solution, it's worse than Debbie's double dipping.

If you really want to take the bull by the horns, ask Debbie if she can help you in taking the platter out. When you and Debbie get to the kitchen, ask her politely to please not double dip. Explain that by doing so she's making the shrimp unappetizing for some of the other guests: "Debbie, I'm sure you didn't even know you were doing this, but . . ." The key is to do this quietly and privately.

Dealing with Friends Who Are Separated or Divorced

Separation and divorce are an ugly time for the couple and for the couple's friends. You want to remain friendly with both parties but are faced with a problem: As the friend trying to entertain, whom do you invite? It's stressful.

So relieve yourself of the stress.

The next time you're faced with this question, explain to both people that you simply don't want to have to make a choice between one or the other, so you're inviting them both. If they can both be there together, great. If not, let them decide who's coming and who's not. At least you've let them know you care for both of them.

POTLUCK OR GROUP PARTIES

Starting an informal potluck tradition is a wonderful way for a group of friends or relatives to sustain their bonds over time, since the responsibility is a shared one and the party's success is something everyone can bask in. For example, over the past few years we've helped organize several monster clambakes on Martha's Vineyard. We dig a pit in the sand, line it with old iron cannonballs saved just for this purpose, and build a huge fire in the pit to heat the cannonballs. When they're red hot, we remove the fire and fill the pit with rockweed, lobsters, corn on the cob, onions, sweet potatoes, crabs, and anything else we can think of. Then we cover it all with a big canvas tarp and let the food cook for three hours.

We've had as many as seventy-five people show up for the event. They all contribute with money, food, and brawn. By the end of the evening, black bags filled with garbage are loaded into each SUV. When we leave, you wouldn't know any event had ever taken place.

There's no way one or two people could pull this sort of party off. For our clambake to be a success (and it must be, because people are always asking when we're going to organize the next one), it takes the willingness of everyone to pitch in.

20

DINNERTIME

Emily Post once wrote: *"All the rules of table manners are made to avoid ugliness. To let anyone see what you have in your mouth is repulsive; to make a noise is to suggest an animal; to make a mess is disgusting."* Viewed objectively, the act of eating is inherently a somewhat, well, gross activity. Think about it: The key to good eating etiquette is to bite, chew, and swallow without offending the people around you. Of course, none of us are bothered by our *own* eating habits—but when the guy across the table takes an enormous bite of hamburger, chews with his mouth open, or talks with his mouth full, the result is disgusting, plain and simple.

Nowhere are poor table manners more evident than at dinner. But good table manners aren't something you can simply switch on when the occasion warrants. Instead, they need to be practiced every day—even if you're dining on pizza alone in your kitchen—so that they become an ingrained habit.

ETIQUETTE IMPERATIVE
How Do You Look to Others?

If you're not sure how you look when you eat, try placing a mirror on the table one night and watching yourself. Believe me, the effort is worth it. Nothing unimpresses quite so quickly as bad table manners and sloppy eating behavior.

THE THREE MOST-ASKED QUESTIONS
ABOUT TABLE MANNERS

1. How should you hold and use your knife and fork? To begin with, don't hold your knife as if you were going to stab someone, or your fork and spoon like you would grip a shovel. To cut your food, if you are right handed you will most likely hold your fork in your left hand and your knife in your right hand. Place the butt of the handle of the fork in the palm of your hand with the tines facing down. Place your forefinger on the back of the handle while grasping the butt with the remaining three fingers. Then grasp the side of the fork with your thumb. Now you can hold the fork firmly. Do the same with the knife: butt of the handle in your palm, forefinger along the back of the knife, grasp the handle with the remaining three fingers and the side of the knife with your thumb. To use a spoon or a fork tines up, balance the utensil in your right hand, resting it on your crooked first finger and the V between your thumb and first finger. Use your thumb to grip the spoon or fork.

Then it's a matter of the correct technique of cutting and then raising food to your mouth: the American style (in which the diner cuts meat with the fork in his left hand and then puts his knife down and switches the fork to his right hand to bring the cut meat to his mouth) or the continental style (in which the fork always stays in the left hand). Either style is acceptable. Do what's most comfortable for you. The key is to get the food from your plate to your mouth without making a mess.

2. Can you put your elbows on the table? The real issue here is how to sit at a table and not look like a slob. If you sit at the table hunched over your plate, leaning on your elbows and shoveling food into your mouth, then the "no elbows on the table" rule is the least of your problems. So, for no other reason, I don't put my elbows on the tabletop. It isn't practical to eat with them on the table.

Between courses, however, when I'm conversing with a companion, I may lean toward the table with my elbows propped on the edge of the table and my hands clasped. Leaning forward in this fashion is one way of showing you're paying attention to the person you're with.

Bottom line: Use common sense. An elbow resting gently on the table between courses shouldn't offend anyone. The one exception to this is when you're a guest. Whether it's a meal at your in-laws' home or a fancy, highbrow dinner party, before you start using the table as an elbow rest, take a look at the other guests and follow their example.

3. What's the correct direction to pass food at a table? Pass to the right. The reason for this rule probably lies in the fact that we live in a right-hand world. When you pass food to the right, you automatically place the dish in the receiving person's left hand. They can then easily serve themselves with their free right hand. (If the dish is especially heavy or large—like a salad bowl, for example—you may want to offer to hold it for the person on your right while she serves herself.)

Passing in one direction also prevents a logjam from happening as platters or baskets come at you from both directions.

When to Pass to the Left

When plates of food are passed around the table, they are passed to the right. But what happens when you are at a table of eight or ten people and the person two seats to your left asks for the bread?

Pass the bread to the left. Making it go the long way around the table would be ridiculous.

ETIQUETTE IMPERATIVE
Your Most Important Task as a Guest or a Host

To return to Emily's observation at the start of this chapter, if you think about making choices at the table that let you avoid being ugly, repulsive, or disgusting, you'll most likely display very good table manners. But the real task of the host and the guest is to be a good conversationalist, a good neighbor, and a good participant. Be sure to talk with the people on either side of you at the table. Participate in conversations by asking questions and making pleasant comments, but don't try to dominate the conversation or impose your views on others, and steer away from controversial topics. Remember, the goal is for everyone to have a lively and fun time.

A QUICK JOURNEY THROUGH A FORMAL DINNER

Arriving at the Table

If you're a guest, look for your place card. If there isn't one, wait for the host to indicate where you should sit.

When you get to your place, remain standing and offer to hold the chairs for the women sitting to either side of you. Once the hostess has taken her seat, or as the host sits down, you may sit.

The Lowdown on Holding Chairs

Women have repeatedly told us they do like it when men do nice things like hold chairs for them. Yet, more than 40 percent of the women answering the 2011 Post Survey say men never hold a chair for them and only 14 percent say men always hold a chair for them. Seems to me those numbers should be reversed. Here's an opportunity for you to look awesome to your wife, significant other, or date.

Immediately place your napkin on your lap. Don't tuck it into your shirt or belt or shake it out to unfold it. Just lay it on your lap.

If you don't know the people seated on either side of you, introduce yourself (for tips on introductions, see Chapter 10, Meeting and Greeting). Depending on how big the table is, you should also nod and say hello to any other people across from you or in your vicinity.

The Place Setting

Intimidated by all those glasses and all that silverware? Not to worry: They've actually been placed with great care to make it easy for you to know when to use which item.

You'll find knives and spoons on the right side of your plate and forks on the left. (The only exception is an oyster fork, which will be on the right. This fork is used for oysters, raw clams, or shrimp cocktail.) The correct order of use is *from the outside in*. This way, the outlying utensils are gradually stripped away as the meal progresses, leaving the utensil for the next course on the outside of the place setting.

Your glassware is set to the right side of your table setting, just above the knives and spoons. The types of glasses used will vary depending on what beverages are going to be served. The glasses are arrayed in the order they are used, from left to right. The water glass—the largest—is on the far left. To its right comes the red wineglass, then the white wineglass, followed (in theory) by a Champagne glass and an aperitif glass. Of course, that's a lot of glasses! It's more common to have a water glass, a red wineglass and/or a white wineglass arranged from left to right.

The bread or butter plate and butter knife (if there is one) are set above the forks on the left side of your place setting. The butter knife is typically placed on the edge of the bread plate.

At a restaurant, if you don't order a particular course the waiter will remove the utensils that would ordinarily be used for that course, so you will have the proper utensils for the next course on the outside of the place setting.

136 | Social Life

The Tie Flip

Every now and then I'll see a guy flip his tie over his shoulder just before starting to eat. It's like a neon sign flashing "I'm a sloppy eater, look at me!" Don't flip the tie. Instead, practice eating carefully, taking a small amount of food on your fork or spoon so you don't dribble food on yourself.

DURING THE MEAL

Wineglasses

Do hold the red wineglass by the bowl. It's easier to balance it that way, and the warmth from your hand won't affect the wine. However, always hold your white wineglass by the stem, to prevent your body heat from taking the chill off the wine.

Tipping the Soup Bowl

Yes, you *may* tip your soup bowl to spoon up the last bit of soup. At a formal dinner, tip the bowl away from you and fill your spoon with a motion that moves your spoon away from your body—not to be pretentious, but to avoid splattering your clothes.

Leaving the Soupspoon

At the completion of the soup course, if the soup bowl is a shallow one, leave the spoon in the bowl with the handle pointing to the right. If it's a deep bowl and there is a plate under it, place the spoon on the edge of the plate, again with the handle pointing to the right.

It's Just Plain Gross

When the first edition of *Essential Manners For Men* came out, I went on a book tour. I was meeting with one group of women in San Francisco and I asked, "On a first date if a man chewed his food with his mouth open, would he get a second date?" A loud "no" echoed through the bookstore. Yet, 45 percent of the women responding to the 2011 Post Survey said the men they eat with chew with their mouth open sometimes or all of the time. Look in that mirror. If it's you, this is one habit you'll want to change.

When to Begin Eating

There are two opposing schools of thought about when to start eating. Emily believed in enjoying a meal while it was still warm. Following this philosophy, when you're with a group of friends in a relaxed situation, it's acceptable to begin eating once at least three people have been served. In a more formal situation or at a business meal, however, you should wait until everyone has been served or until the host or hostess says something like, "Please start right away. Don't let your food get cold waiting for ours to be served."

If you are the host, once three people have been served, let them know that it's all right to start. As Emily noted, it would be a shame to let that delicious food start cooling just because every guest hasn't been served yet.

Salt and Pepper

When you need salt and/or pepper, always ask for both. Likewise, if someone asks you for "the salt," pass both.

Don't salt or pepper your food until *after* you've tasted it. Once I mistakenly salted split pea soup before tasting it. Turns out it was salty to begin with. After I finished salting it, it was inedible.

Resting Your Utensils

If you want to take a break from eating, simply place your knife and fork on the plate with the tip of the knife and the tines of the fork positioned at the top of your plate. Tines up or tines down? Knife blade facing one way or the other? It doesn't really matter—just do it neatly and you'll be fine.

And *never* put a dirty utensil directly onto the table.

Sopping Up Sauce

I can't stand to leave a really good sauce sitting on a plate. Break off a small piece of bread, then use your fork to push the bread around in the leftover sauce and bring the morsel to your mouth.

Cutting Meat, One Bite at a Time

When you're cutting your meat, slice off one bite-size piece, eat it, then cut the next piece. Unless you're preparing a plate for a young child, don't cut a whole steak into bite-size pieces and then start eating.

Excusing Yourself

If you need to leave the table during the meal, gently fold your napkin so that any soiled parts are covered, then lay it on the table to the left of your place setting. Do the same thing when you leave the table at the conclusion of the meal.

Nose Blowing

A quick wipe in an emergency is okay, but true nose blowing should happen in the restroom.

Placing Utensils When You're Finished

At the end of each course, picture your plate as a clock. Then place your knife and fork on your plate side by side in the four-o'clock position. Don't get anal about whether your dinner partner "made a mistake" because he or she placed the fork above the knife or left the blade of the knife facing away from the fork. If you are that focused on other people's faux pas, then you're missing the real point of good table manners and formal dinners, which is to enjoy the company you are with.

Dessert Arrives

As the host, you've made the choice to serve dessert at the table. You cut the first piece of Black Forest cake and place it on the nearest plate. As you do, some frosting gets on your finger. *"Man, it looks good,"* you think to yourself. *"What about just a quick lick?"* Don't do it. Either wipe your finger on a napkin or keep serving as if nothing happened.

Saying "No, Thanks" to Coffee or Wine

If wine or coffee is being served and you don't care for any, don't turn your glass or cup over. Simply tell the server, "No, thank you." If you are served anyway, simply leave the glass or cup alone and go back to your conversation, which is much more important anyway.

AT DINNER'S END

As a guest, don't take it upon yourself to call a close to the evening. As you've done throughout the evening, take your cues as to the proper time to leave from the other guests and from your host.

When the time comes for you to bid farewell, thank your host for a special evening with all the warmth and sincerity you can muster. Also, make sure to say good night to the people who were sitting on either side of you and to the other diners who were near you at the table.

Finally, when you get home that evening, take a few minutes to write a brief thank-you note of three to five sentences to your host. Address and stamp the envelope, and put the note in a place where you'll see it and remember to mail it the next morning. Your host will appreciate your thoughtfulness, and you will have cemented your reputation as an engaged, gracious dinner guest—ensuring that you'll get invited back again.

21

THE HOUSEGUEST
FROM HELL

You know who I'm talking about: that out-of-town visitor who leaves a trail of belongings around the house, expects to be waited on, leaves his or her children with you as though you were running a babysitting agency, puts down roots in your sofa, or—worst of all—doesn't know when to leave.

Of course, spotting the things that someone *else* is doing wrong is easy. It's a lot more difficult to admit the ways in which you may be ruffling your hosts' feathers when you are the overnight visitor. As you read about the following houseguest-from-hell behaviors, take a look in the mirror and ask if you see yourself in any of these situations.

THE ETIQUETTE OF VISITING:
BE CLEAN AND HELPFUL—AND SHARE THE REMOTE!

According to our survey, making a mess is the biggest factor that turns an ordinary houseguest into the Houseguest from Hell. Topping the list of making a mess complaints were scattering dirty clothes on the floor, leaving shaving stubble and hair in the sink, failing to hang towels on the towel rack, leaving the bed unmade, using dishes and then not washing them, and failing to wipe shoes before entering the home.

Other issues besides leaving a mess that sparked our respondents' ire included the following:

Being a Sloppy Guest

The sloppy guest fails to respect the host's home and in many cases grosses out his hosts with his uncouth behavior. Complaints centered on:

- Putting feet up on the furniture
- Walking around in various states of undress from no shirt or just in underwear to wearing nothing at all
- Not washing hands before handling food
- Peeing on the toilet seat or missing altogether
- Not using air freshener in the bathroom when needed
- Not flushing the toilet
- Clipping their nails in the living room or kitchen
- Drinking directly from the container rather than using a glass

Being Disrespectful

The complaints in this category centered on guests who simply go over the line, by:

- Expecting the host(ess) to wait on them hand and foot
- Bragging and acting self-centered
- Ignoring the host or hostess
- Inviting friends over without asking first
- Showing up with an unannounced companion, child, or pet
- Being downright rude
- Staying too long

The Toilet

In our survey, one out of ten houseguest complaints focused specifically on toilet issues. The majority of comments focused specifically on the issue of not putting the toilet seat down. Take note: Given that this issue is no longer mentioned as a major concern in the daily life survey, it seems men are more prone to this frustrating behavior in other people's houses than in their own. Add in complaints about issues around flushing and aim, the toilet is the single biggest "mess" respondents identified.

Usurping

When men use things without asking or just assume whatever they are thinking of doing is okay, they irritate their hosts. Just because your host has a beautiful guitar in the corner doesn't mean you can just pick it up and play it without first asking. One respondent was aghast that a house-guest used her toothbrush. Other acts of usurping include plopping yourself down in the host's favorite chair, raiding the refrigerator, wearing the host's clothes, and taking a bike or, worse yet, a car without permission.

Being Unhelpful

Complaints included failing to help to clear plates from the table, not pitching in with the dishes, and never offering to help with household chores.

Hogging the Television

In particular, our respondents complained about houseguests who turn into couch potatoes upon their arrival, insist on watching nothing but sports, or who sit clutching the remote, not allowing anyone else near it.

Not Saying "Thank You"

Failure to say "Thank you" popped up repeatedly. "Thank you" comes in three forms. You can bring a house present upon arriving for your visit (see page 145), you can say "Thank you" sincerely when you are getting ready to leave, and you can send a thank-you note after you return home. There's also a fourth way: Remember to be complimentary and say "Thank you" throughout your stay.

A Sample Thank-You Note

Dear Dan and Jan,

I can't thank you enough for the great time I had visiting you at the shore. The cricket match was so unexpected and made for such a fun day. I had no idea the sport could be so riveting!

Dan, you were right—the beach and the swimming and the scenery make your place a terrific getaway! I'm more relaxed now than I have been in months.

Jan, the party you threw on Saturday night was fantastic. And the pie! Dan has probably told you that I'm a sucker for strawberry pie, and yours was the best I've ever tasted!

Thank you both for showing me such a great time. I hope you can make it out to Milwaukee for a visit sometime this fall.

Best to you both,

Tony

THE FIVE KEYS TO A SUCCESSFUL VISIT

These five guidelines will spell the difference between a successful visit and a friendship turned sour.

1. **ESTABLISH A DEFINITE TIME LIMIT FOR THE VISIT WHEN THE INVITATION IS MADE.** Friendly Fred thought he was doing the right thing by inviting his old college friend Bill to stay with him for a couple of weeks. Bill had recently lost his job and was thinking about moving to Fred's city.

   "It'll be like old college times in the dorm," Fred told Bill.

Now, a month later, Furious Fred is ready to hogtie Bill and throw him out on his ear. Bill has moved in lock, stock, and barrel, and Fred can't budge him. He even tried announcing that he was going away for a week, and Bill countered by saying that he would be happy to water the plants and feed the fish while Fred was away. It was the least he could do, he acknowledged.

Fred made the classic mistake: He extended an invitation with no preset time limit. If you invite someone to stay at your home, *set a definite time frame at the time you make the invitation.* Conversely, if you're planning a visit and your host tells you to stay "as long as you like," gently explain that you really have to be back home at a certain fixed date.

Here's how Fred *should* have worded his offer to Bill:

"Why don't you come stay with me for a few days? You could stay until next Wednesday morning. We'll have the weekend to catch up, and you can check out the job opportunities on Monday and Tuesday. By Wednesday, you should have a good idea whether there is anything here worth pursuing."

Then, midway through Bill's visit, Fred says, "Hey, Bill, I'm trying to set up my schedule for Wednesday. How about if I give you a ride to the train station on my way to work?"

If Bill replies that he's thinking of staying longer, then Fred needs to dig in his heels and say, "That's great, and I've enjoyed our visit, but Wednesday is as long as I can have you stay here, Bill. If you're planning on staying longer, you'll need to find another place. I'm sure you understand."

Take Them Out to Dinner

One alternative to the house present is to offer to take your hosts out to dinner. Make the offer when you are invited or before you arrive so the hosts have time to plan accordingly. If you aren't familiar with the town, ask them for a recommendation and then call and make a reservation right away. Don't make it the host's responsibility to organize the dinner.

2. **BRING A HOUSE PRESENT.** People frequently ask me, "Do I have to bring a present every time I'm visiting someone overnight?"

   "Yes," I answer. The gift needn't be grandiose—just something that says, "Thank you for inviting me into your home." For an overnight or weekend stay, plants or flowers are always a good idea. Another gift that I really like is a coffee-table book—one that's fun to look at with lots of pictures, either on a subject you know your hosts are interested in (a photo history of cricket, for example) or on a subject you're interested in and that you think your hosts would enjoy learning more about (such as a book on the most beautiful hill towns in Tuscany). Finally, a box of chocolates is also nice—provided your hosts aren't on a diet. I don't recommend bringing a bottle of wine. Wine is an appropriate gift for a dinner party, but not as a houseguest present.

3. **GO WITH THE FLOW.** Today's the day: Tony has finally made his long-promised visit to Dan and Jan at their vacation house at the New Jersey shore. It's the first morning after his arrival, and the sun is already high in the sky when he ambles down the stairs, his head filled with thoughts of the beach, swimming, bikinis, and lots of nothing to do.

   "Hey, Tony, you lazy slug," Dan says, putting down the morning paper. "Today's the day: The cricket match finals are only thirty minutes from here, and we've got front-row seats. You've got just enough time for a shower and a cup of coffee, then we've got to hit the road."

   Cricket matches? What happened to the beach and the swimming and the bikinis?

   Answer: *When in Rome, do as the Romans do.* When you're a houseguest, you go with the program—cricket matches and all. Suddenly, Tony sees his plans for fun in the sun vanish. Within a few minutes, though, he is showered, caffeinated, and ready to go: "So, Jan, what's cricket all about? If you guys are into this sport, there must be something to it. Tell me more . . ."

4. **MAKE AN EFFORT TO CONTRIBUTE.** Simple acts of contribution make all the difference in the world—like helping with the dishes, straightening the furniture in the living room before you go to bed, wiping down the bathroom after showering and/or shaving, or offering to chop vegetables before dinner. In particular, make an effort to help with the tasks that are a part of your visit.

   If you stay for several days make an offer to help contribute to the cost of the food and beverages. Even if the offer is turned down, the fact you made it will be greatly appreciated.

5. **THANK YOUR HOSTS TWICE.** The first time you thank them is when you're ready to leave: "I had a great time," Tony tells Dan and Jan, as the taxi that will take him to the airport idles nearby. "I can't thank you enough for your hospitality—not to mention the great food. You'll have to let me return the favor by hosting you at my house in Milwaukee. There's no beach, of course—but there are some restaurants I know you'll love!"

   The second thank-you should be sent by mail as soon as you arrive back home.

Gift Suggestions for a Longer Stay

When the visit will be longer than an overnight or weekend, you may want to consider a larger gift:

- A breakfast basket from a local gourmet shop that could include pancake mix, bacon or Canadian ham, and real Vermont maple syrup.

- Fixings for an ice cream sundae party (especially good if kids are involved). For a visit with friends in the Adirondacks, we filled a basket with a variety of syrups and toppings, a couple of cans of Reddi-wip, and a small ice cream maker.

- A set of monogrammed beach towels. Great for a summer vacation visit to the beach or if the hosts have a pool.

MEETING THE PARENTS

Oh, those awkward first moments when you're meeting the parents of your significant other for the first time. Should you introduce yourself to them? How do you greet them—with a hug or a handshake? And what should you call them?

Here's the scenario: Dan and Jan are planning to visit Jan's parents for the weekend—the first time Dan has ever met them, much less stayed with them.

The front door swings open.

"Jan, honey, you made it! We're so glad to see you . . ." and on it goes: hugs and kisses for Jan. Then it's Dan's turn.

Jan starts out: "Mom, Dad (remembering that you always address the more important person first when making an introduction—and in this case, even though Dan is the light of her life, she shows ultimate respect for her parents by talking to them first), I'd like to introduce Dan Petrified to you."

Next, Jan turns to Dan and says, "Dan, these are my parents, Tim and Heather."

And now Dan faces the big question: Is it "Tim" and "Heather," or is it "Mr. and Mrs. Intimidating"?

It's Mr. and Mrs. Intimidating, no question about it. Dan leads off with the formal, ultra-respectful form of address. He says, "I'm pleased to meet you, Mr. and Mrs. Intimidating." Ninety-nine times out of one hundred, Mr. or Mrs. Intimidating will respond, "Oh, Dan, we're so glad to finally meet you. Jan's told us so much about you. And please—it's Tim and Heather."

22

SOCIAL MEDIA

There's a huge universe of interconnectivity going on out there through social networking sites like Facebook and Twitter. Even your smartphone can get you into hot water when you text message personal information. Just remember: Everything online is public and permanent. There is no putting it back once the genie is out of the bottle. If you don't think so, just check out the news for the latest public figure who's used social media to convey something private and suddenly had the whole world witness it. Lives and careers have literally been shattered because someone broke the cardinal rule of online communication: *Don't put anything out there that you wouldn't want the whole world to see.*

SOCIAL NETWORKING

Unfortunately, it's your image out there, even if it's your friends who screw it up. They can post pictures of you that you would prefer don't get seen. You can ferret those pictures out and at least remove the tags that identify them as you. More proactively, you can contact the person who posted the photo and request they remove it. In addition, please show your friends the same consideration you want them to show you and be careful about tagging photos and posting photos of them.

Friending

Growing your circle of friends is a natural part of socializing in the real world and that translates to a significant part of the online world as well.

You can make a request to be someone's friend. Just remember, there's no requirement for them to accept the friend request, much less acknowledge it. Don't pester someone who hasn't responded. Let it go.

There will be times when you wish to end an online friendship. When that time comes, it's okay to unfriend or unfollow the person. Different services handle unfriending in different ways, so check to see how your service handles it. Usually the friend count simply drops by one; no message is sent.

ETIQUETTE IMPERATIVE
Breaking Up Is Hard to Do

At least that's what the song says. Some people have come to the conclusion that breaking up really isn't that hard to do now that you can hide behind the electronic brick wall and not have to face the person you're dumping. No way should you ever use an e-mail, a text message, an instant message, or any other electronic message to do your dirty work. It was a personal relationship—end it in person or at least with a personal phone call.

If you break up with someone, should you unfriend them? Maybe yes, maybe no—you may have friends in common. When in doubt, you may even consider discussing the friending situation with your ex before you simply pull the plug on her.

Sexting—For Your Eyes Only. Not.

If ever there was a reason to understand that texting is a public means of communication, sexting is it. And at the worst possible instance, it will go public. Images of you nude or in compromising positions that you send to that special someone "for her eyes only" suddenly get passed around for all your friends and anyone else to see. Once it's out in cyberworld, you can't stop it. Just read the headlines.

THE WORLD OF ONLINE DATING

My wife and I were sitting in our living room with Seth, a good friend who is recently divorced. As we talked his phone chirped. A little later it chirped again. It turned out he had registered with an online dating site, and he was astonished at how he had begun making contact with people. It was our first time having an up-close look at the world of online dating and meeting people. What became immediately clear from Seth's experience was how the same manners, the same underlying way to approach someone in person, apply in the online world as well: Be considerate, respectful, and honest.

Where the online and the in-person worlds of meeting people seem to differ is that the anonymity of electronic communication provides a more relaxed "getting to know you" phase. In fact that first moment of getting to know you happens safely and anonymously as prospective people peruse your profile.

Here are several tips to use as you check out different online dating sites:

- Use a reputable service; check it out before signing up.

- Don't give personal information (cell number, personal e-mail, physical address)—only use the e-mail provided by the service.

- Respect privacy—don't divulge others' names and screen names.

Your Profile

One tip stands out above all others when creating your profile: Be honest. Small fabrications and embellishments can haunt you when you get to the in-person stage. As sure as the sun rises, you will be caught in the lie, and then what does that say to the person you've finally connected with about your trustworthiness? And the implication of one white lie is: What else would you lie about? Hmmmm . . .

Phase One: First Contact

You've read a profile, and you think this person may be someone you'd like to get to know better. The next step is to make contact electronically. The great thing about e-mail is it's a safe means of communication for both of you. You can use it to check each other out and get to know more about each other's likes and dislikes, interests, and habits. At this stage just be careful not to write things that could be misinterpreted or turn off the possibility of a relationship before it's even gotten off the ground.

- If you don't hear back from someone, try again. After two strikes move on.

- Be selective—you don't have to respond to everyone who contacts you.

- Be polite when responding—use a greeting and mention something from the person's profile to show you actually read it!

- The e-mail stage is for asking questions and finding out about each other—so use good e-mail etiquette to make a good impression.

- Don't gossip about friends or coworkers, or share proprietary information from work.

- Be careful introducing controversial topics: sex, politics, religion, personal finances, obscene jokes. Don't assume you know the other person's feelings or beliefs.

- Pace yourself . . . don't say it all in one e-mail.

Finally, after e-mails have gone back and forth, you will arrive at a point where you'd like to take the next step: talking on the phone. So in an e-mail ask her: "Would it be okay if I called you or if you prefer, can I send you my phone number?"

Phase Two: Talking on the Phone

So far all you've had to go on are the words she's used e-mailing you. With a phone conversation, you're upping the ante. Now you and she will experience personality defined not only by words but by quality of voice (see Chapter 8). Be careful to be upbeat and positive when you talk. Before you pick up the phone, put a smile on your face and get focused. Don't be watching TV, fixing dinner, or doing anything else that might distract you from the call. And when she answers, make those first words you say positive and confident. Let her know right up front that you're excited about this next step in getting to know each other. "Hi, Samantha, this is Bill. I've been so looking forward to talking with you. . . ."

When to Quit the Playing Field

It's okay to casually "date" or interact with more than one person while you are still playing the field. But once you begin actively dating a person or when the relationship is a go, then you should take down your profile from dating sites.

Phase Three: Meeting in Person

The phone conversations have gone as well as the e-mail communications. You're sensing that the time is right to take the next step: meeting in person. So you ask her and she says, "Yes." Now everything is on the line. It's not just your voice, it's your actions, your appearance, and your words that all add up to make a good impression. Take care with the following to get that first face-to-face meeting off to a good start:

- Suggest meeting at a public place where other people will be around.

- Keep it simple: Each of you can pay your own way on the first "date."

- If you do set a date, show up! It's a commitment that must be honored.

- Be on time.

- Dress appropriately and put effort into your appearance.

- Turn off your cell phone.

- Greet her respectfully—stand up when she approaches, look her in the eye, say your name clearly, and offer to shake her hand. Do it nice and firmly, two or three shakes, and then let go.

- Be a good conversationalist. You've learned a lot about her in the e-mails and phone calls, so spend a few minutes before you meet up thinking of some questions you can ask as conversation starters.

- Remember to listen, too. Conversation should be 50/50—50 percent you, 50 percent her.

- When it's over, let it be over. You've both got a lot to think about, considering if you want to see each other again or not.

- FOLLOW UP! No matter how the date went, call or send a thank-you e-mail the next day.

- If you want to take it further, take your time.

"Maybe This Isn't a Good Idea . . ."

Following up after that first meeting is very important whether you want to try to take it further or not. If you do, great; be encouraging. But if she's not right for you, let her know, but do it gently: "It was fun meeting you but I don't think we have that much in common after all. I wish you the best."

Remember, even if you want to continue, if she backs off, then respect her wishes and let it go.

ONLINE GAMING

The world of gaming has exploded. You can literally compete with and get to know people from around the world. Because of that electronic brick wall, you may be duped into thinking the rules of normal social interaction don't apply. They do.

- Check the site's rules and be prepared to follow them or don't play.

- Winning is easy, losing isn't. Be a good winner and a good loser.

- Think before you hit the Enter key or start keying. People hear your tone in your words.

- Trash-talking, jeering, and cheering can all be okay as long as they are in line with good sportsmanship.

- Keep appointments, communicate clearly, and treat common facilities with respect and consideration.

23

THE BIG DAY:
THE WEDDING

Whether you are a guest or a participant, we're talking about a very special occasion. Ideally, a wedding is a once-in-a-lifetime event. That makes this day incredibly important. When you're the groom, you can multiply that last statement by a thousand. I'll talk about the groom's role a little later on. For the moment, however, let's focus on whenever you've been invited to a wedding as a guest. In everything you do—from responding to the invitation, to purchasing a wedding gift, to wearing the right clothes—it's all about how you act and how your actions either make or break you.

If you're attending the wedding with a date, your significant other, or your spouse, the stakes are even higher. My totally unscientific personal observation is that women do a transference thing at weddings. It seems like during a wedding every woman—no matter what her relationship situation is—dreams of herself as the bride. And that fact raises the importance of weddings to all-time highs. You need to take this event very seriously and recognize just how important it is to the woman you are with, even if you'd rather be home mowing the grass.

THE GUEST: WHEN YOU ARE INVITED

You can't miss it when it arrives in the mail—the handwritten address, the special shape of the envelope, the thick, high-quality paper. It's addressed to you personally.

Mr. John Sullivan
123 Main Street
Riverdale, CA 93656

Can You Bring an Uninvited Guest?

Now John faces an interesting problem: He and Marcia have been dating for about six months. Typically, when a couple is in a serious relationship but still living in two separate locations, each person will receive a wedding invitation. Since Marcia knows the betrothed couple as well, John wonders if maybe she received her own invitation. She hasn't said anything to him about it, so John calls up and asks her. Nope.

Can John go ahead and ask Marcia to go with him to the wedding?

No. No exceptions.

Here's why: In planning the wedding, the bride and groom carefully set the number of guests they are inviting. If just one person brought an uninvited guest, it wouldn't cause a problem. If five or ten or twenty people brought uninvited guests, it could play havoc with the table space, the amounts of food being served, the quantities of beverages being consumed, and ultimately the budget. So no exceptions: If Marcia isn't invited and John's invitation is addressed just to him, he shouldn't bring her and he shouldn't ask if he can bring her.

On the other hand, there are a couple of scenarios in which Marcia could come along.

1. The bride might specifically invite both of them by including Marcia's name on the envelope, too. The following example shows how a wedding invitation is addressed to two people who live together but who aren't married:

Mr. John Sullivan and Ms. Marcia Goodfellow
123 Main Street
Riverdale, CA 93656

2. The bride may have known John is in a serious relationship but wasn't sure of the woman's name. In this case she either includes a note with the invitation asking John to bring a plus one or she addresses the inner envelope to:

Mr. John Sullivan and Guest

Now, technically, when the invitation is worded this way, John doesn't have to bring Marcia. He could bring his good friend Ralph or another woman. In his response he should indicate the name of his guest, so the bridal couple will know her name.

ETIQUETTE IMPERATIVE
Bringing Your Kids to a Wedding

If your children are not invited to a wedding and you can't get child care, do not show up with your kids. If you do get stuck, make sure you let the bride know you can't attend, and express your regrets pleasantly: "I'm so sorry we can't come, but I simply can't find anyone to take care of Joey and Sally."

If the invitation lists your child(ren)'s names on the envelope, or if it says, "Mr. and Mrs. John Sullivan and family," or if each child receives a separate invitation, then the children are invited and may attend the wedding. If the invitation simply says, "Mr. and Mrs. John Sullivan," then the kids are not invited. Don't bring them.

Exactly What Does R.S.V.P. Mean?

At the bottom of the invitation are four letters: R.S.V.P. These letters stand for *Répondez s'il vous plaît*, which is French for "Respond if you please" or "Send an answer." This imperative holds whether you're planning to attend or not.

Usually the invitation includes a preaddressed, stamped return envelope along with a little card with a space for you to write your name and mark "Accepts" or "Regrets." Use it.

If there is no response card, then write your response on a note card and send it. Wedding responses used to follow a highly formal structure that would send everyone running to *Emily Post's Etiquette* to make sure they were doing it the "right" way. In today's world, however, no matter how you word your response—as long as you aren't rude about it—your answer will be just fine.

Do I Have to Give a Wedding Gift?

Yes. This is true whether you attend or not.

If you're wondering what to give the happy couple, Dan and Jan have probably registered at several stores and, most likely, online as well. Phone Jan's mother, one of the attendants, or someone else close to the couple and ask. They expect these calls, so it's neither awkward nor embarrassing for you to ask them about this sort of information.

Remember, too, that just because Dan and Jan have registered somewhere, it doesn't mean you have to give them a gift from their registry list.

Buy a gift prior to the wedding day. Have it delivered to the bride's home, to her parents' home, or to the couple's home if they are already living together.

What Should I Wear?

The three "acceptable" dress choices for male wedding guests all include some form of a tie. At my brother's wedding in a field behind my parents' house in Vermont, some men came without a tie and still looked presentable. But from the point of view of what you *should* do—of what will make you look "sharp," and signal your respect for the specialness of the occasion—wear a tie. You can always remove your tie if the situation warrants it.

And don't argue about it before the wedding. Just do it.

Here are the three options:

A TUXEDO. This attire is for the really formal wedding in the evening. If you don't own a tuxedo and it's expected, rent one. You wear it with a special shirt with French cuffs and a bow tie. It used to be that only a black bow tie was acceptable, but today men wear a variety of colored and patterned bow ties with matching cummerbunds. (I have a great pink one that always elicits a few "oohs" and "ahs" from the ladies.) If the invitation indicates "Black Tie Optional," then you have the choice of wearing a suit or a tuxedo.

A DARK SUIT. This is acceptable at any wedding: day or evening, formal, semiformal, or informal. The only time you shouldn't wear a dark suit is when the invitation specifies Black Tie. Then, if you plan to attend, you really must wear a tuxedo. A dark suit is worn with a conservative (white, blue, pink, yellow, or striped) shirt and a tie.

A BLUE BLAZER OR DARK JACKET AND GRAY FLANNELS OR LIGHT PANTS (SUMMER ONLY). Traditionally, the blazer or jacket was an option only at an informal, daytime wedding. Today, though, you'll see it worn as an alternative to the dark suit, especially when it's coupled with a pair of dark gray flannel pants. The only time I would not opt for a blue blazer or jacket would be at a formal daytime or evening wedding.

ETIQUETTE IMPERATIVE
Wear a Tie

....

Wear a tie with a jacket or suit. This is a really important occasion for the bride, the groom, their families, and the person you are with. Honor them by wearing a shirt and tie with a jacket or a suit.

....

The Importance of Being Attentive

Weddings are incredibly special days, when the woman you're with really wants you to be near her, paying attention to her, making her the most important person in your life—just as the bride is the most honored person in the room on that particular day.

Forget the game on TV. Forget hanging out with the guys. Today, even though it's not your wedding, make it a special day for both of you by being her prince.

According to the survey, the men who accomplish this are absolute heroes. Here are some of the things, our female respondents tell us, that heroes do at weddings:

- Act as if she is the most fascinating person in the world.

- Show particular sensitivity to children, elderly people, and anyone feeling left out of the circle.

- Talk to the other guests and be interested in what they have to say.

- Have eyes only for her and make her feel like a very important part of his life.

- Whisper sweet things in her ear when other people are around.

- Include her in conversations with others she may not know.

- Make a concerted effort to socialize.

Reread this list and memorize it. If you do these things, you'll make this day very memorable for your date. And that's a very good thing for everyone.

ETIQUETTE IMPERATIVE
Dance!!!

When my daughters read the galleys for this book, they were emphatic about dancing. "Put lots of exclamation points after this word," they implored me. "Tell men how important dancing is to women." Now they've told you.

By the way, this holds for nonweddings, too. Even on your average night out, if there's dance music playing, dance with your date. It's a sure bet to make her happy.

When to Leave

Eating fast and then leaving immediately doesn't cut it at weddings. In fact, "cutting it" is the signal for when it's okay to leave—after the cutting of the cake, that is.

Thank You

As always, whenever you are a guest, before you leave you must be sure to thank the hosts. Make a point of seeking out the bride and groom (if they haven't left already) as well as the bride's parents and the groom's parents. Thank all of them for including you at this wonderful event.

Then, the next day, sit down and write each of them a thank-you note. Two or three sentences is fine. Technically, this note is optional, but it is an incredibly nice thing to do.

THE GROOM

Getting Engaged

There are as many different ways of getting engaged as there are stars in the sky. There's really only one piece of advice I can give you on this point: It's a big moment and a big commitment, so be sure of what you're doing. Beyond that, how you pop the question is up to you. Just remember: The more complex a plan you concoct, the more chance there is for something to go wrong.

My nephew showed real class and imagination. As he and his intended walked across the Brooklyn Bridge, he stopped, went down on bended knee, and proposed to her. Personally, I would have tied some dental floss to the ring and held on to the other end for dear life just in case the ring slipped.

"Should I Ask Her Dad for Permission?"

In the final analysis, individual circumstances will determine whether you should ask permission, either alone or with your intended, or if you should simply announce your plans together. Be respectful of the culture and traditions of your future wife's family. This will help you decide on the most appropriate course of action.

The Jumbotron

We've all seen it. Seventh inning at the ball game and a special message flashes on the Jumbotron: "Sally, will you marry me?" You go down on bended knee, and the camera pulls in for a super close-up of Sally to catch her response for the whole world to see. If she's expecting it, great. But if it's a surprise, boy, is she in an awkward spot. I mean, what if her answer is a "no" or "not yet"? Better to ask this important question in private.

Picking Groomsmen

Think family and think close friends. You'll have to negotiate with your fiancée as to how many attendants you both will have at your wedding. Her brothers and your brothers are candidates, as are your closest friends. One way to honor a brother or friend who doesn't make the short list is to ask him to be an usher or a reader at the ceremony.

The Bachelor Party

The bachelor party is one of those infamous anachronisms to which more legend has been created than facts can attest to. Having one is entirely optional. It's usually hosted by the best man, but the groom or the groomsmen together can host if they prefer. Contrary to popular opinion, a bachelor party is not an opportunity for the groom-to-be to sow one final bunch of wild oats before he's tied down for good. It is an opportunity for the groom and his close friends to spend some quality time together, and perhaps escape the craziness of the final wedding preparations for a few hours.

Be creative when planning this gathering of men. When my nephew got married, as the best man his older brother arranged a bachelor outing consisting of a canoe trip down the Connecticut River along the Vermont/New Hampshire border. He rented canoes and sleeping gear, and laid in an abundance of supplies. They had a great and memorable time.

And that's what it's all about.

The Rehearsal Dinner

Tradition has it that the bride's family paid for the wedding and the groom's family paid for and hosted the rehearsal dinner—a celebration the night before the wedding. The rehearsal dinner followed the rehearsal of the ceremony, which was planned for the late afternoon on the day before the wedding. Then all the attendants and participants in the ceremony gathered for a meal. Spouses, significant others, and even dates were invited to the dinner, as well as the officiant and his or her spouse. Some people argue that out of town guests are invited as well, but that is not necessary. When I was married, our out-of-town guests were invited to a separate party hosted by good friends of the bride's parents.

Who Pays for the Wedding?

Who pays for what is no longer strictly along traditional lines. Each couple and their families need to have an open and frank discussion about who is contributing to the wedding and what is a reasonable amount for each. There is no bottom-line dollar requirement for a wedding today.

Today's Groom's Responsibilities

Today's groom often participates to a much greater degree than grooms of the past. Most important, brides and grooms may be the ones paying for their wedding. Because he may have a direct financial stake in the event, the groom often takes a full partner's role in planning the size and type of wedding. This is a dicey task: He'll have to balance his bride's dreams with the reality of the budget.

He should spend time with the bride making selections for gift registries. Since the gifts the couple receives are for both of them, their registry should include items they are both excited about and that fit their lifestyle and their tastes. The only way to accomplish this is if the groom takes an active role in picking items for the gift registry. And remember, registries can include items that previously might have been considered out of bounds: camping equipment, contributions to the honeymoon, or charitable donations in lieu of gifts to the couple.

He shares in the task of writing thank-you notes. In today's world, the bride and groom are both likely to have full-time jobs. Writing thank-you notes is mandatory, and they should be written within three months of receiving a wedding gift. Helping do it is a great way to say to your intended that you are a team and you share responsibilities.

He attends meetings with caterers and other service providers.

And he helps determine the invitation list.

My mother-in-law-to-be gave me just one task at our wedding: Be at the church on time.

I was.

The Receiving Line

After making sure you're actually present for the ceremony, your next duty will be to stand in the receiving line if there is one. Frankly, I don't remember doing this—but my wife assures me I was there and has the photos to prove it. It's an opportunity for your families' friends and relatives to wish you well.

Smearing Cake in Your Bride's Face

Don't do it.

Tossing the Garter

Brides toss the bouquet to a group of unmarried female guests and attendants. The person who catches it is thought to be the next to get married. Similarly, the groom removes a garter, which is discreetly positioned on the bride's leg, and then, like the bouquet, tosses the garter to a group of unmarried men with the same supposed result as the bouquet. Just do it tastefully.

Toasts

One of the most terrifying ordeals any man will face is standing up in front of a crowd and giving a toast. Often this high-pressure moment occurs after the *toaster* is already *toasted*. Mix a person's natural nervousness with some alcohol and an unplanned toast, and you have a recipe for disaster. Since you can't do much about the nervousness, and since I'm not going to tell you to hold off on all Champagne until after the toasts, you've got only one recourse: Write down your toast on paper a couple of days ahead of time, and then practice it a few times—out loud. Remember to bring the paper with you.

Here are a few other tips:

- Keep your toast short. Short is very good from everyone's point of view.

- Always start by thanking everyone for coming. You can even make a special point of thanking the people who came from farthest away.

- Thank her parents. Tell them how happy you are to be part of their family.

- Thank your parents.

- And then honor your bride.

That's it—your official duties are done. Enjoy the evening with your bride. Go with her to visit with the guests. Then dance the night away, at least until it's time to leave.

OTHER MANLY ROLES AT A WEDDING

The Best Man

Ideally, the best man is supposed to be the stable, level-headed rock on whom the groom—who is expected to be totally frazzled on the day of his wedding and usually is—can rely on to help him get ready and get to the church on time. (I said "ideally." I know of some best men who needed more help than the groom.)

Besides arranging the bachelor party (see above), the best man is also responsible for making sure the wedding rings make it to the altar. He should either give the wedding rings to the ring bearer just before the ceremony or bring the rings up to the altar himself, where, at the appropriate time, he hands them to the person performing the ceremony.

Whatever else you do as best man—*don't forget the rings*.

Another major best man responsibility is to toast the bride and groom at the reception. The toast should be an expression of good wishes to the happy couple, of thanks to the groom for being such a great friend, and of joy at the fact that the groom has found such a fantastic person to share his life with. Save your wild stories of the past for the occasional "guys' night." If you are nervous about making a toast—and many best men are—be especially careful about drinking before you give your toast. Alcohol has caused many a well-planned toast to degenerate into a long-winded embarrassing monologue.

When You're a Groomsman or an Usher

As one of the groomsmen, you may be invited to a couple of prewedding parties. For the big event itself, you'll be asked to dress in specific clothes. Often this involves renting a tuxedo. If so, the groom will let you know exactly what you need to rent. In addition to the wedding gift, you'll also probably be asked to chip in on the groomsmen's presents, either to the groom or to the couple.

Groomsmen and ushers arrive early for the ceremony and show guests to their seats. One usher may be asked to stand next to the guest register, if there is one, and ask guests to sign it as they arrive.

As an usher or groomsman you'll be expected to escort female guests to their seats at the wedding ceremony. If a woman is unattended, simply offer her your arm and lead her down the aisle. If she is with a husband or significant other, then you still offer to take her arm and he follows behind you. Ask her if she is a guest of the groom or the bride. The bride's guests traditionally sit on the right side of the aisle, and the groom's guests sit on the left. If one or the other side simply has significantly more guests than the other, then it is okay to seat people so both sides fill up evenly.

You may also be asked to perform specific tasks, such as rolling out an aisle runner. If that's the case, you'll practice doing so at the rehearsal. Once the guests are seated and the procession is about to start, ushers will take a seat themselves. Groomsmen will assemble with the wedding party and prepare to proceed up the aisle. Following the ceremony, you should pick up leftover programs or belongings, and be generally helpful to guests who need assistance or directions to the reception.

At the reception, make sure you dance with the mothers of the bride and the groom, as well as with the maid of honor and the bridesmaids, and keep an eye out to make sure the bridesmaids are having a great time.

Finally—have a great time yourself!

PART THREE

ON THE JOB

24

TOP THREE ISSUES FOR WORK LIFE

Now that you're an expert on situations involving daily life and the social world, prepare to move back to square one—because the work world presents a completely different set of etiquette problems, which are critically important to your welfare and your future. How you handle yourself on the job will have a major impact not only on your own performance, but also on the morale and productivity of your colleagues and the trajectory of your career. When you treat your coworkers with consideration and respect, you are helping your business become a happier and more efficient enterprise. Fail to show consideration, on the other hand, and you become a business liability.

THE THREE MOST ANNOYING ISSUES IN WORK LIFE

The most annoying thing men do at work is treat women as second-class citizens or as sex objects. The second has to do with men who act in a superior way to their colleagues, both male and female. These behaviors can often be traced to the fact that the worker in question simply "doesn't like" the coworker he is putting down or feels threatened by the coworker.

Whatever the reason, these attitudes are a mistake. Whenever you act as if you're "better than" your colleagues or put other people down, you can't avoid being rude to them in the process. The third annoying thing is a lack of general manners.

Negative Behavior #1: Male Chauvinist Attitudes Persist

One type of male with a superior attitude stands out above all others: the male chauvinist. His condescending, deprecating attitude toward women generates harsh criticism from women in our surveys and by itself is the most mentioned problem behavior in the workplace. Women are treated as sex objects. They are given menial tasks. They are ignored. They are interrupted. They are stared at. They are treated as less intelligent. The list goes on. Here's what women say in their own words:

> "Most men that I've worked with seem to act as though they think they are superior to women in terms of authority and ideas simply because they are male. Most, if not all, regard women as sexual objects and define women's credibility as a function of their attractiveness."

> "Some men are patronizing and condescending, mostly toward women but sometimes toward those with less experience or more 'junior' status. It doesn't seem to be generational either. Some men in my own age group do this and yet some older ones do not. When it happens to me, it is quite annoying and makes working with that person very difficult."

> "Sexism, especially in a male-dominated computer science field. It isn't over-the-top blatant sexism but strong surprise from men that a woman is able to help them create software. Also it's uncomfortable when new male clients assume that every woman must be a secretary or an assistant rather than a college-educated computer programmer."

> "Talking to my boobs; assuming I'm less intelligent than a male counterpart."

"A male peer of mine introduced me as his 'right-hand girl' and that was the extent of his introduction. He never told my name at all. The men on the team were introduced by name."

"Many workplaces may still be a 'man's domain' but that doesn't excuse you to treat women like second-class citizens. Whether you're the CEO or the janitor, you'll get a dazzling smile if you hold open the door as you walk through or offer any other professional courtesy you'd offer to a man in the workplace. Not asking for more—just the same."

If you see yourself in any of these comments it's time to do a careful personal assessment and change your behavior.

Negative Behavior #2: A Superior or Demeaning Attitude

Whether you are putting someone else down or your behavior says, "I think I'm better than you and/or more important than you," then you are acting in a superior manner.

Sometimes a superior attitude will be overt and very obvious. Other times it may be more subtle, but just as destructive. Again, if you recognize yourself in any of the following behaviors, it's time for a little soul-searching:

- Are you macho?

- Are you a know-it-all?

- Do you act like you own the place?

- Do you assume that because a person has a "lesser" position, they're not as smart as you?

- Are you late?

- Do you fail to listen carefully?

- Are you "one of the boys"?

- Do you refuse to do your share?

When you put other people down, you are directly assaulting their sense of themselves by demeaning them, belittling them, and trying to tear down their self-esteem and belief in their own value. It doesn't matter whether you do these things intentionally or not: If you can see yourself in any of the behaviors I'm about to describe, you need to think long and hard about what that behavior says about you—and about how you can start to change.

- Do you try to dominate others?

- Do you shout and bully?

- Do you use false terms of endearment?

- Do you flirt on the job?

- Do you interrupt colleagues?

- Do you ogle and stare at attractive coworkers?

Negative Behavior #3: Lack of Manners

Be assured that your coworkers will take notice when good manners are lacking. At the Emily Post Institute, we've gotten some astonishing stories about people's poor manners, such as the men (there seem to be a number of them out there) who like to sit at their cubicle desks, take off their shoes and socks, and start clipping their toenails. Or the worker who attended a mandatory seminar and sat in the back of the room reading the newspaper the whole time. Or the sales associate who was riding in an elevator full of people following a sales call, and turned to his supervisor and started talking about the deal they just negotiated. Or even the group of male employees who wanted to know if it was really necessary to leave the toilet seat down in a unisex bathroom.

The interesting thing about manners in the workplace is that often problems center on the little things rather than major faux pas. The trouble is the little things add up. Flash points that got the most complaints in the surveys included the following:

- Sloppy table manners

- Lousy phone and e-mail etiquette

- Not making introductions properly

- Simple failure to say "please" or "thank you"

- Bad hygiene

- Inappropriate clothing

THINGS MEN DO WELL IN WORK LIFE

On the positive side, people have great respect for coworkers and business colleagues who treat them as equals, listen to them, praise them when they deserve it, are polite, and get the job done. If you do these things consistently and sincerely, you'll find these behaviors will make a real difference in the quality of your business relationships.

These behaviors really come down to treating your business associates with consideration, respect, and honesty. Underlying these most basic ways of treating each other is being thoughtful. Time and again when asked to comment on the impressive things men do at the office, the examples cited were grounded in a thoughtful attitude.

"It's always great when someone on the tech team brings in coffee for everyone on an early Monday morning. It creates a good atmosphere and general happiness."

"Compliment a female coworker on her job. Recommend a female coworker for an upcoming job or assignment."

"Listen to women with whom they work. Give them credit for their ideas and work collaboratively on projects."

"Admitting fault, accepting responsibility, and not repeating the error; giving direction in a comfortable nondemeaning noncoercive way; receiving direction in an amiable and cooperative way."

"I enjoy working for a man who does not talk down to me but can treat me as if I have something to add to the business."

"It has been an honor when I've worked for a man who is professionally mature and leads with focus and respect. This leader knows how to motivate his team and often has a humility that is sometimes lacking in those in lower positions."

Interestingly, manners do matter, even at work. Even in the gender-neutral work world, the little things you do are appreciated: Offer to hold a door, help lift a heavy object, pick up lunch, get a cup of coffee, share a box of tissues, introduce a colleague, and/or include a colleague in water-cooler talk.

BUSINESS RUNS ON RELATIONSHIPS

Businesses need people who know how to get along with and bring out the best in other people despite any differences they may have—people who know how to listen and learn, and who are able to put aside their personal likes or dislikes and pull together to produce the finest possible work. In short: *Businesses need people who know how to build relationships—not tear them down.*

The work world revolves around relationships. Your work skills may get you in the door for a job interview or make a sales pitch. But it's your *people skills*—your ability to connect with an interviewer, a prospective buyer, or your boss or coworkers—that will drive your success.

I owned an advertising agency, and whenever I'd hire someone, I'd tell that person right up front that I have three inviolable rules, which if broken will lead to dismissal. Two of these rules have to do with productivity.

Rule number three is the "people rule": *You must be able to get along with the other people in the office.* If you can't, then I'll be forced to choose between who can stay and who has to go—and you might not like my choice.

This third rule illuminates the key differences between your work life and your nonwork life. In the business world, no matter what your job, you are going to have to accomplish the following:

- Work with people with whom you otherwise might not choose to associate

- Listen and take instruction or guidance from someone with whom you don't always agree

- Do things in a certain way, even if you don't always believe this is the best way to do them

HOW OTHERS SEE YOU

Suppose that you work at my advertising agency, and you don't like a certain coworker very much, or you think the sales rep for one of our suppliers is an idiot, or you cringe every time you have to do work for a particular client. From your perspective, your behavior toward these people is understandable and defensible: Your cold-shoulder, abrupt, and uncommunicative treatment of your fellow employee is your way of saying, "Stay out of my space—I may have to work here but I don't have to deal with you"; your superior attitude toward the supplier arises from your impatience at his plodding way of reviewing every purchase request; and your readiness to argue over every question, comment, or objection the client makes is your way of emphasizing that your solutions are the "right" ones.

From my perspective, however, your behavior tells a very different story: Your rudeness toward your coworker is resulting in lost productivity for both of you; your superior attitude toward the supplier is causing him not to go the extra mile for our company; and your ongoing arguments with our client are the first step on the road to losing his business.

In the workplace, my perspective on your interactions with these people directly affects your potential success. It's not just about how you see yourself. Your success depends on how others see you.

COPING WITH LAYOFFS

The dreaded pink slip causes angst in the workplace both for the unfortunate person laid off and for the person still left with a job.

If you've been laid off, take care with your leaving. As tempting as it might be to shoot off a few choice words, it's better not to burn any bridges. You never know when the person you just castigated will be hiring again or has moved on to another business and suddenly you're applying to her for a job. Whenever possible, keep potentially valuable connections.

You can let your fellow employees know you've gotten a pink slip. Try not to engage them in negative conversation about the company or your boss. It will be difficult for them to split their loyalty between you and their jobs.

If your colleague has been laid off, you can certainly commiserate with him. But don't engage in trash-talking your boss or the company. No good can come from it, and it may boomerang to hurt you. A better approach would be to offer any help you can. Do you know anybody you might introduce him to in his job search? Can you help him strategize possible alternatives for careers? Can you simply offer friendship and a willingness to stay in touch or spend an evening together as friends?

25

Five Cardinal Rules for Your Job Interview

1. Don't Be Late

Mr. Job Applicant-Come-Lately asked, "I was twenty minutes late for one job interview, but I was only five minutes late for another. I didn't get either job, and I think it was because I was late. Is this fair?"

"Five minutes, one minute, it doesn't matter. No job. No excuses, no exceptions," I answered firmly.

"Even just five minutes late?"

"That's just the way it is: If you're late for the interview, don't expect to be offered the job."

Above all others, there is one inviolable rule when interviewing for a job: Be there on time. Your arrival is your first opportunity to make a good impression on your prospective employers. If you keep your interviewer waiting even a minute or two, you'll most likely never recover from the bad impression you've made.

Lateness is never a mark of importance. Rather, it is a mark of rudeness, arrogance, or disorganization—personality traits you certainly don't want people to associate with you. Anytime you're late, whether you are a job applicant or a CEO, whether it involves work or play, you're being disrespectful of the people you're supposed to be meeting.

Here's how to avoid the problem: Go to the site a day or two before the interview. Learn how long the trip will take. Then factor in some extra time just to be on the safe side. If there is no security checkpoint, go into the business itself and introduce yourself to the receptionist. That way you'll know exactly where the office is. This also gives you a chance to check out what people in the office are wearing so you can be sure you're dressed appropriately for the interview. If there is a security checkpoint, then simply observe the dress of the people entering the premises (see Job Interview Tip #3: Dress One Notch Up).

On the day of the interview, plan to get there five to ten minutes ahead of time. If you arrive really early, you can always stop somewhere nearby for a cup of coffee. In a worst-case scenario when you find yourself stuck on a commuter train that has stalled between stations or you're at a dead standstill in a monumental traffic jam, this is the perfect time to use your cell phone. Call and explain the circumstances that have made you unavoidably delayed. Apologize sincerely, give an estimate of when you will arrive, and ask if they would prefer to reschedule. If you're lucky, you may salvage the situation.

2. BE PREPARED

The job interview is not about your job skills; it is about your personal skills. Your job skills are what got you in the door—you wouldn't even be there if the company didn't think you had the skills and the potential to do the job. What really makes the difference is how well you connect with the interviewer(s). To make that connection, you'll need to draw on your full array of personal skills:

- How you stand, sit, dress, talk, listen, and respond to the interviewer
- How confident you are
- How knowledgeable you are about the company

- How comfortable you are talking about yourself

- How well you project an image that matches the type of person the company is searching for

Getting ready for a job interview is like prepping for an exam. Learn everything you can about the company you are interviewing with. Call ahead to find out the pronunciation of key names; use their Web site to research the company mission statement, policies, principals, and the products or services they offer.

A Job Interview Is a Two-Way Street

Remember, a job interview is a two-way street: Not only is it an opportunity for a company to learn what type of person *you* are and whether they think you'll fit their corporate culture—but it's also an opportunity for you to learn if *they* are a good fit for your needs. Ask yourself if the interviewer is the type of person you'd really like to work for. The same goes for any other people you meet during the interview. Consider carefully, too, if the job tasks they've defined for you are tasks you are interested in doing.

3. DRESS ONE NOTCH UP

There are very few hard-and-fast, do-it-this-way rules in this book.

This is one of them.

Okay, so you were working for a dot-com where the dress code embraced T-shirts, jeans, and no socks. But those days are over, and now you're applying for a job at an insurance agency.

Different culture. New rules. *Their* rules. So be sure you dress for the part. In fact, for the job interview, you should always dress just a little sharper than the norm for that corporate culture. If the guys typically wear slacks and a shirt but no tie, you should wear a coat and tie. If they are wearing sports jackets and ties, wear a suit. The idea is to always dress one notch up.

What Not to Ask

The initial job interview is not the time to ask how many vacation days you get, what kind of benefits are offered, and how many holidays you get. The time to ask these types of questions and negotiate a salary is after you've already been offered the job and are deciding whether or not to accept the offer.

4. SMILE, SPEAK CLEARLY, AND LOOK YOUR INTERVIEWER IN THE EYE

People who smile exude confidence. If you can show your interviewer that you are confident (but not cocky), you will also be showing him or her that you have the ability to represent the company as a confident, can-do person. So *smile*. Not a big crazy grin, just a relaxed, confident smile.

Speaking clearly is also vital. If the person conducting the interview can't understand you, then he/she will assume that coworkers, prospects, clients, suppliers, and the general public won't be able to understand you either. Translation: no job.

Finally comes the importance of looking people in the eye. I'm disconcerted when I interview someone who can't meet my eyes. Their gaze wanders to the left, to the right, to their lap, their fingers, anywhere but at me. Again: no job.

Review the body language tips in Chapter 27 to make sure you present the best image possible.

5. THANK THEM TWICE

The first thank-you should come at the end of the interview. When the interview is finished, stand and shake hands with each person in the meeting. While shaking hands, look that person in the eye and thank him/her simply and directly. For example, you might say: "Thank you for the opportunity to interview for the job. I've enjoyed meeting you and am looking forward to hearing from you soon."

When you get home that evening, compose a thank-you note, essentially repeating what you said in person. An hour or so later reread it. Look for any possible errors in punctuation, grammar, word usage, spelling, names, and titles. Then ask a roommate, spouse, significant other, friend, parent, or other relative—anyone you trust—to read it for you as well. Make sure it is mistake free.

Then, and only then, print out a final version on your personal stationery and put your thank-you note into a matching envelope, place a stamp on it (don't use a postage meter), and deposit it in the mail.

Thank-You Note Tips

This is your final opportunity to show your prospective employer how well you communicate.

- Since this is a business communication, you should type it.

- Keep it short—no more than one page.

- You don't need to restate your qualifications in the letter. The company already has your résumé and your application.

- If anything came up in the interview that focused on a particular strength you have, you can reiterate it here. Example: "During the interview you mentioned the importance of building a presence on the Web. I had the opportunity to help build the Youth Corps Web site last summer. I have checked with Tom Miller, the director, and he would be happy to talk with you about my work. His number is 802-555-1221."

- End on a positive note: "Thank you for your time and interest. I look forward to the possibility of joining your staff."

- Send your thank-you note either by postal mail or by e-mail. E-mail can be especially effective when a decision is imminent; they'll be sure you understand the importance of a thank-you. Send an e-mail when you know the preferred means of communicating at that company is via e-mail. Use regular mail when you want to show you know how to present a polished image. And if you are unsure you can always elect to send an e-mail thank you and then follow it up with a thank-you note sent through the mail.

FIVE INTERVIEW QUESTIONS
YOU SHOULD BE PREPARED TO ANSWER

Setting aside some time in advance to practice your answers to the usual questions you can expect in a job interview will give you an edge of confidence during the interview itself. This confidence will translate into a comfortable, positive attitude, which will reflect well on you and could even prove to be the decisive factor in your getting the job. The best way to practice is to say your answers out loud in a normal tone of voice. So here we go:

- Why do you want a new job?

- What do you know about our company and why do you want a position with us?

- What are your strengths?

- What was the hardest thing you faced in a previous job?

- Tell me about yourself.

A Bonus Question to Prepare For

Where do you see yourself in two or three years? This question lets you explore how the job you are applying for fits into your goals for your career. Be prepared to give a big picture answer.

FIVE QUESTIONS TO ASK DURING AN INTERVIEW

- Why is this position available?

- Which of the job's responsibilities are the most important ones?

- What do you consider to be the strengths of your company?

- What are the main problems facing the staff today?

- How would you describe the successful candidate for this job?

Thank You Goes Both Ways

Corporate responsibility includes thanking you, too, for your time interviewing and acknowledging your application. When businesses don't do these things, ask yourself if you want to work for that kind of company. The interview is a two-way street.

BEWARE YOUR ONLINE PRESENCE

I know a young man who applied for a summer job recently. At one point during the interview, the interviewer asked him if they could spend a couple of minutes looking at his Facebook page together. There on his wall was a photo a friend had posted of him. His friends thought it would be funny to place a bunch of empty beer bottles around him while he slept on the beach and then take a picture and post it. The interviewer was not amused.

There are too many stories of inappropriate images and comments on social network sites that end up costing jobs, promotions, or friends. Make sure you police your own images and information regularly, and ask yourself how this would look to my boss, a client, a prospect, or a potential employer. It's not enough to police your own images; you need to vet the images people tag with your name as well.

26

BUILDING BETTER
RELATIONSHIPS

Emily Post always made it quite clear that the essence of etiquette was about building the best possible relationships with everyone in your life. In her first book on manners, *Etiquette*, published in 1922, she noted that some people did not believe etiquette was important in business—and then cautioned her readers not to toss this valuable business tool aside:

A certain rich man, whose appointment to a foreign post of importance was about to be ratified, came into the corridor of a Washington hotel and stopped to speak with a lady for a few moments. During the whole conversation he kept his hat on his head and a cigar in the corner of his mouth. It happened that the lady was the wife of a prominent senator, and she lost no time in reporting the incident to her husband, who in turn brought the matter to the attention of certain of his colleagues with the result that the appointment did not go through.

People watch how others conduct themselves in their various relationships. We all get judged by our "people skills" as well as our "job skills," and in business the final choice often comes down to this "people skills" judgment.

People skills are both the knowledge of manners and the ability to use those principles to resolve etiquette issues. Emily also recognized the importance of mastering the *principles* of etiquette rather than just mastering a superficial display of manners, and used no less a gentleman than Abraham Lincoln as her prime example:

> Because Lincoln's etiquette was self-taught he was no less masterly for that! Whether he happened to know a lot of trifling details of pseudo etiquette matters not in the least. Awkward he may have been, but the essence of him was courtesy—unfailing courtesy.

NEGATIVE BEHAVIORS HURT RELATIONSHIPS

Here are some of the most common work-related "negative behaviors," along with suggestions on how to change them for the better. These annoying behaviors tear down relationships, cause hard feelings, and, if left unaddressed, can ultimately lead to reduced productivity, lost profits, and high employee turnover.

Words Matter

What you choose to say and how you say it will be remembered by other people and will influence how they view you.

The most obvious negative example of this is the way people—especially young people, it seems to me—litter their speech with the "f-word." Their choice of language leaves me unimpressed: They're certainly not convincing me that they're grown up; and if they think the shock value of this word is going to get me to pay attention to them, they should realize that the "f-word" lost its shock value long ago. Not only am I not going to pay special attention to them because they use that word but it may well cause me to tune them out.

Obscenity and coarse language have no place in business; they do nothing to enhance communication and everything to enhance your image as a person with a foul mouth. But you can also ruffle feathers simply by using words that might be normal for you but that are offensive to someone else.

....

Inappropriate Touching

Tom, Jane's boss, walks into her cubicle to speak with her about a new assignment. As the conversation ends, Tom stands and reaches forward with his left hand. "Thanks for taking on this assignment. I really appreciate it," he says and gently squeezes her shoulder.

It's just a friendly touch—nothing more. In Tom's eyes, his gesture is simply an attempt on his part to show that he truly appreciates the effort Jane is making.

Jane, however, sees it another way. To Jane, Tom's arm squeeze is just plain weird. *"Why did he do that?"* she thinks to herself. *"I've never seen him touch a male employee other than to shake his hand. Why didn't he just shake my hand? What's going on here? Is he making a pass at me? Is there more to this than he's letting on?"*

WHAT TO DO: Something as simple as touching a woman can lead to major interpersonal problems, not to mention a lawsuit. If you feel you want to connect with a colleague in a physical way, *reach out and offer to shake hands* as you thank him or her for taking on the assignment. Stay away from all other forms of touching in the workplace.

Terms of Endearment

"Honey," "darling," "babe"—there are loads of these terms. The speaker who uses these terms of endearment may think he's just being friendly. But to the coworker who is their recipient, these terms can come across as depersonalizing, inappropriately informal or forward, or even a form of unacceptable flirting.

Tom gets up to leave Jane's office. No touching, he reminds himself.

Instead, he says, "Thanks, sweetie." *"Sweetie?"* Jane thinks to herself, as she stares at his receding back. *"I'm not your 'sweetie'—I'm Jane. J-A-N-E."*

WHAT TO DO: If you wouldn't use a certain word when you're addressing a male coworker, don't use it when you're talking to a woman either. As a general rule, avoid all terms of endearment in the workplace. People have names. Use them. You won't go wrong.

Coercing

Coercing is a classic "ends-justify-the-means" action. Coercing is a way of getting people to do things they don't want to do: "Come on, Jack—let's take the company car and go out to lunch. What are you, a wuss? No one will ever know!"

In his mind, the "ends" of going out to lunch, rather than eating at the company cafeteria, clearly justify the "means" of getting Jack to disobey company regulations.

WHAT TO DO: Coercing is unacceptable, period—whether it involves coercing a coworker to borrow a company car for personal business or demanding that a colleague use illegal accounting practices to cover up a billion-dollar loss. Follow the rules, and let those around you know that you expect them to do the same.

Swearing, Shouting, and Using Coarse Language

It doesn't matter whether or not the phrase is offensive to *you*—what matters is if it is offensive to someone else with whom you're interacting.

WHAT TO DO: Whenever I speak with people, I try to take into account their different backgrounds and cultures, as well as the geographic regions they hail from. I need to ensure that my word choice doesn't get in the way of my goal—which is to deliver my message effectively and build the best relationship possible with my audience.

Being Domineering

You can be domineering with your words, your actions, or your appearance. When the intent of your words is to put down the other person rather than discuss the issue at hand ("You don't know what you are talking about!" "How could you say something so stupid?"), you've crossed the line from arguing to being domineering.

The tone in which you deliver your words—especially if you shout—can be just as domineering as the words you use. Finally, body language can be incredibly intimidating and domineering as well—particularly if it involves standing over or standing very close to another person.

WHAT TO DO: When discussing a problem with a coworker or business associate, outline the problem in a neutral, nonpersonal way, using words that *critique* rather than words that criticize. Stay calm and keep your voice under control, your tone modulated and steady. Anytime your voice betrays anger or frustration, the person you're speaking with will inevitably begin reacting to your emotional state rather than to the issue at hand. Be cognizant of your body language as well: It won't help to control your tone of voice if you're "shouting" with your body.

Ogling

"I try not to stare," you protest—"but sometimes she wears clothes that are designed more to catch a man's eye than to do work in."

I know it can be hard, especially when a particularly good-looking woman is in the room. And some of those outfits *are* eye-catching. But that doesn't change the fact that staring or ogling is inappropriate behavior in the workplace.

WHAT TO DO: It may be that the good-looking colleague isn't aware or doesn't care that she's crossed the line—but the other people in the room (both men and women alike) will care. They expect you and everyone else to be focused on the job at hand and to be able to concentrate even if there is a distraction. Your attention needs to be on the information and knowledge each person brings to the task, and not on their physical attributes. When you're at work, learn to focus on work. Save the looking for after hours.

Ignoring Other People's Opinions

When I talk with businesspeople around the country, all too often I hear complaints about men failing to listen, or men ignoring other people's opinions, or men not giving credit when credit is due. In the team environment of today's corporations, this sort of behavior has become more noticeable and disruptive than ever before. Building strong, cohesive teams is an integral part of business today.

This means learning to function within a collaborative team environment rather than maintaining a competitive, "doing-my-thing-alone" attitude. For example, let's say the software team at xyz.com has been asked to develop a new app. The development process is complex and focus is critical to the team's success—but if team members are distracted by feelings of frustration over the attitudes of other team members, they won't be able to focus properly. When Jill writes a weekly report that makes it sound like the latest innovation is her idea alone, the other team members become resentful and suspicious of Jill—("I'll bet she's angling for a promotion")—and in turn less cooperative.

WHAT TO DO: Listen carefully to what others are saying—and show that you're listening by asking probing questions or building on their train of thought. Acknowledge others when they make a contribution: "Great concept, Jill. What can we do to enhance it further? Ideas anyone?" This will keep the focus on the work and not on personal slights.

Interrupting

Interrupting is cutting another person off at the knees, plain and simple. It says to the other person: "Sorry, Jack, but whatever you have to say isn't worth the time it takes to say it."

WHAT TO DO: Start listening. Stop interrupting.

CHOOSING TO GET ALONG

One fact that differentiates work life from daily and social life is that you don't get to choose your work colleagues. They come with the job—which means that to succeed at your job, you have to get along with people you might otherwise choose not to associate with.

This challenge is especially great at the start of any new job. Whenever you put a man into a strange environment, such as a new workplace, there's a natural tendency for him to switch into a defensive, competitive mode. Add to the mix some people whom the man doesn't "take to" or whom he feels uncomfortable around, and his defensiveness can all too easily shift over into demeaning actions and/or a superior attitude—the two leading sources of workplace friction.

Understandable? Possibly. Defensible? No.

Be aware that whenever you enter a new work environment, your natural defenses are automatically going to kick in at first. Focus on these points to overcome this and immediately begin forging positive new relationships:

- Focus on being a member of the team.

- Listen—really listen—to what your coworkers are saying.

- Concentrate on doing the tasks that your education and experience have prepared you to do.

- Work on finding value in your colleagues and learning from them.

- And finally, like Lincoln, let the essence of you be courtesy—unfailing courtesy.

27

OFFICE COMMUNICATIONS

If you learn only one lesson from this chapter, let it be this: *You can't take back your communications.*

"I didn't say that."

(Yes, you did.)

"I didn't mean that."

(It's what they heard.)

"Please ignore my previous communication."

(Right!)

Whether you say it or you write it, once a message has been sent, it becomes a reflection of who you are. Jumbled, incoherent thoughts and rambling communications make you appear disorganized and ignorant. Typos, poor grammar, or embarrassing word choices make you look sloppy, imprecise, and foolish. The recipient's feelings of annoyance, frustration, or derision suddenly become the focus rather than the message you really intended to communicate.

No matter what form of communication you use—face-to-face conversation, video chat, e-mail, IM, memo, letter, fax, or telephone—if you satisfy the following four criteria, people will focus on your content and not your inadequacies:

- Is it clear? (Have you said what you intended to say?)

- Is it unified? (Have you stuck to your point?)

- Is it coherent? (Will the communication make sense to the recipient?)

- Is it focused? (Could you have said your piece more succinctly or written it more concisely?)

Unfortunately, with the business world in hyperdrive these days, the clarity, conciseness, unity, and coherence of corporate communications seem to be diminishing. Here is a review of the different mediums used to communicate in today's fast-paced business world and some tips on how to make the most of them.

FACE-TO-FACE

In some ways, face-to-face communications are the most difficult of all, while at the same time you have the best chance of success. When you're talking face-to-face, people can hear and see you.

You have the best chance of your message getting through because you use facial expressions, gestures, and nonverbal cues such as tone of voice and body language. These can enhance your communication and underscore meaning. When you only use your voice, such as when talking on the phone, you lose the benefit of facial expressions and gestures; when you write a note, such as an e-mail, you lose the benefit of vocal expression as well.

Case in point: Bob is slated to give a major presentation to his company's board of directors. This is it—his chance to shine or to crash and burn. He's run through his PowerPoint presentation a dozen times already to make sure the equipment operates without a hitch. But he should also make a point-by-point check of his *own* equipment.

- Is his voice confident and clear or does it quaver from nervousness?

- Does he speak concisely or does he tend to repeat himself three times every time he makes a point?

- Does he speak at a regular pace or does he race through his presentation at ninety miles per hour?

- Is he comfortable with the appropriate lingo or does he mispronounce words?

- Does he move around the room as he talks or does he grip the podium like a vise?

- Does he engage members of the audience with his eyes and with hand and arm gestures, or does he stand like a statue, eyes fixed on his notes?

- Is he dressed appropriately for the occasion? (I once forgot my belt and had to keep my jacket buttoned throughout the presentation.)

Here are some pointers on how to make your face-to-face communications more effective:

Speaking Volume

Shouting your words won't give your argument more strength. Talk in a conversational tone. If you're going to use a microphone for a presentation, practice with one ahead of time to give yourself a chance to get used to hearing your own voice amplified.

Tone of Voice

There's nothing more conducive to putting your audience to sleep than speaking in a monotone. Speaking in an animated voice helps the listener discern the important parts of what you are saying. Your tone of voice can either imply, "I don't give a hoot about what I'm talking about," or it can say to your audience, "This is really important—listen up."

Rate of Speech

Ideally, when speaking to a group, you should talk at the same speed you would use when talking with a friend.

Accent

Normally, a slight accent isn't a problem. But if your accent is so thick and heavy that people have to strain to understand what you are saying, then you need to work on reducing it. In the meantime, slow your rate of speech and take care to enunciate.

Body Language

How you look is just as important as what you have to say. Through your posture you can either engage the person you are talking with or you can reject him or her completely. Of course, one's posture alone doesn't necessarily convey an attitude. On its own, crossing your arms and leaning back might not mean anything. But couple it with a curt tone, a scowling face, or tightly pursed lips, and you can almost guarantee that your listener won't be particularly receptive to your comments.

The eyes are powerful communicators as well. If you avoid looking someone in the eyes, it may indicate that you feel awkward about his presence or uncomfortable about what you are saying. If you stare too long into someone's eyes, you may be subtly challenging her authority.

Slouching conveys an impression of laziness or not caring.

The hands-in-pockets posture is more casual, while keeping your hands out of your pockets, perhaps even clasped behind you, projects a more engaged or authoritative image.

Finally, jiggling a foot or knee while sitting can communicate a sense of exasperation, impatience, anxiety, or boredom to the person with whom you are talking.

BUSINESS PHONE ETIQUETTE

Think about how frustrated you become when someone uses a phone inappropriately. Here are some suggestions on how to avoid the most egregious telephone errors at the office:

FACE-TO-FACE VS. PHONE CALL. If you're having a conversation with a person face-to-face, that conversation *should always take precedence over a phone call.* Use the Do Not Disturb feature and route the call to your voice mail. If you don't have a Do Not Disturb feature or an answering device, you may have to answer the phone. In this case, tell the caller that you're busy and will call him back later. One caveat: If you are expecting a call you feel you must take, let the person who is with you know the circumstances in advance and offer to meet with him another time if it would be more convenient.

PLACING SOMEONE ON HOLD. If you put a person on hold, do so for a short period of time—no more than a minute or two at the most. If there's a problem, get back to him and explain the situation briefly. If you are the one being put on hold and the wait lasts more than three minutes, hang up and call back later. (When you do, try your best not to show your annoyance.)

IDENTIFY YOURSELF. There is nothing more frustrating than getting a call and not knowing to whom you're speaking. Always start your conversation by identifying yourself: "Hi, Tom, this is Jim Smith at Aerospace"—or, if you know Tom somewhat: "Hi, Tom, this is Jim Smith"—or, if Tom is a good friend: "Hi, Tom, Jim here. How about lunch today?" If someone calls you and doesn't identify himself, take the first opportunity to say, "Thank you for calling, but I want to be sure who I'm speaking to. You are—?" Don't assume that caller ID is accurate either. A preemptive "Hi, Serena" could be answered, "No, actually it's Jake. Serena's not here right now." "Uh, sorry . . ."

MAKE YOUR CALLS YOURSELF. I know I'll catch flack for this, but I bristle whenever I get a call that starts, "Hello, Mr. Post, this is Thomas, Mr. Jones's assistant at Aerospace. Mr. Jones would like to speak with you. Can you hold a minute while I get him on the line?" There's something fundamentally wrong with this picture. Mr. Jones is calling me and now he's putting me on hold to wait for him. Hey, Mr. Jones, my time is valuable, too. Have the courtesy to make the call yourself and start the conversation on the right foot.

ANSWERING CALLS. Start with a greeting like "hi" or "hello." Identify the place the person is calling. Adding a brief comment that defines what your company is adds to your company's branding every time you answer a call. Then give the caller your name and ask how you can help him. Here's a great example: "Hi, this is Acme Widget Company, maker of the best widgets in the world. This is Bruce. May I help you?"

TRY ANSWERING THE PHONE. If a phone is ringing, don't always wait for someone else to answer it. "Hi, this is Bill Jones at Aerospace. Can I help you?" Mr. Jones just went up ten notches in my estimation. Here he is, the head honcho, and he's answering the phone. I know one CEO who takes a regular turn answering calls at his company's call center. Imagine the pleasant surprise when a person calls with a question or complaint and hears the company's CEO on the other end of the line. And imagine the attitude of the people who work at the call center, seeing their CEO experiencing firsthand the issues they deal with.

TAKE EFFICIENT MESSAGES. When you take a message for a colleague, write down your name, the date and time of the call, the caller's name, company, phone number, and a brief reason for the call. Finally, indicate whether your colleague should return the call or if the caller will call back later.

SPEAKERPHONES. Anytime you are going to use the speakerphone feature, let the person on the other end of the line know right away that he or she is on a speakerphone, and then immediately introduce anyone else who is in the room with you. Have each person say "hello" in a clear voice as you introduce them, so that the caller can identify the voices of the different participants.

If you have a speakerphone at your desk in a cubicle or open office area, avoid using it like the plague. It's hard enough having to listen to people speaking on the phone, but having to hear both sides of a conversation is doubly distracting. In addition, don't just hit the speaker button, dial, and wait for the phone to be answered before picking up your receiver. Everyone in your area has to listen to the *beep, beep, beep* of your dialing, the ringing of the phone, and the voice answering the call before you pick up the receiver. Personally, I'd ban speakerphones from open office and cubicle areas. They're too much of a distraction.

CALL WAITING. Maybe you work at home or in a small office with call waiting rather than multiple phone lines. When you hear that call-waiting beep, ask the person you're talking to if he or she can hold for just a brief moment. Talk to the new caller only long enough to tell him or her that you'll have to call back, then return to the first person and complete your conversation. When your call is done, then—and only then—call the second caller back.

ETIQUETTE IMPERATIVE
Telephone Basics

While the person on the other end of the line can't see you, he or she *can* hear you. If you're not careful, the things you do or the sounds you make can range from annoying to downright gross. When you're talking on the phone:

- Don't multitask.

- Don't chew gum or eat.

- Turn off radios, stereos, and other sound devices.

- Don't sneeze or cough or blow your nose into the receiver.

- Set the receiver down gently.

- Don't engage in subterfuges like having a colleague listen in on the call unannounced.

- Don't interrupt someone who is on the phone with someone else.

"We Can Still Hear You"

Conference calls are great, but beware the mute button. Just when you think the call has been muted and you start commenting critically about someone on the other end, you hear a voice over the speaker: "Tom, you probably don't realize it, but we can still hear you." Here are some other conference call courtesies:

- Don't take a call just before the conference call starts. Be sure you can arrive on time.

- Gather everyone in your location in one room if possible so you can at least see each other.

- Be sure to introduce each person so other people on the call can begin recognizing voices.

- Have an agenda and stick to it.

- Ten minutes before the call is meant to end, announce the ten-minute mark so people can begin wrapping up.

- After the call be sure to send out minutes and information on any to-dos as a gentle reminder to participants.

Smile. You're Live!

Conference calls are a great way to bring a group together while avoiding travel. But they've always lacked the personal touch that being able to see the other person brings. Now with video conference calls so easily available, remember, not only can people hear you, they can see you picking your nose, reading the newspaper, whispering to a colleague, or even sleeping. Be alert, be focused, and be engaged just as you would if the people you were meeting with were in the room with you. They are.

VOICE MAIL

Do the person you are calling—and yourself—a favor: leave coherent messages. "Hi, this is Bill Jones at Aerospace. Tom, I'm sorry I missed you. Could you call me back at 555-1212? I'm calling to discuss . . ."

Keep the description of why you are calling short—two or three sentences at most. Always start your message by stating your name, company, and the number you can be reached at. At the conclusion of the message, repeat your phone number—slowly and clearly. I hate it when a person leaves me a rambling message, tacking on the number only at the bitter end, and then says the number in such a garbled or rushed way that I have to listen to the whole message a second time to get it right.

THE CELL/SMARTPHONE

Cell phones are one of the most useful and one of the most misused tools in business today. The reason is simple: Too many people have lost control of their cell phones. Their thinking goes something like this: *"I've got to have it on all the time because now I can be reached anytime, anyplace—and I'm so important that people need to be able to reach me anytime, anyplace."* One wonders how we ever survived without cell phones. The answer is: We survived just fine.

Control Your Cell Phone: Turn It Off

For those times when you really need it on, save your coworkers from having to listen to your ringtones by using the Vibrate or Silent Ring feature.

That's the long and the short of it. Use your cell phone when you need to use it, of course. But leave it on only when you know that you can answer it without disturbing other people. Be careful of abusing the use of your phone for personal calls while at work. They interfere with your job and your boss will notice.

Move to a Private Area

If you use your cell phone for business in a public place, remember that even though you may not know the other people around you, that *doesn't* mean your conversation isn't disturbing them. And don't even think about talking about confidential or privileged company matters in a public place. Either move to a more private place, or don't make or take the call. It's *not* another person's job to move away from your conversation—it's your job to move your conversation away from them.

Texting

Taking personal calls at the office is something colleagues and bosses alike will notice, but text messages are easy to receive silently. You may think that makes exchanging text messages with your friends while you're at work all right. It's not. Make your personal calls and read and write your personal text messages during your breaks or while at lunch. When you're on the clock, focus on your work.

E-MAIL

I wish I had a dollar for every inappropriate e-mail that has ever been sent to me. If I did, I'd be a very rich man.

E-mail is a great communication tool. Here are five rules to keep it so:

RULE #1: If you can't post it on a bulletin board for anyone to read, then don't send it. I have heard dozens of stories about chagrined e-mail senders who discovered that what they thought was a private communication had become a very public embarrassment—in some cases resulting in lost jobs. Every e-mail is a public document.

RULE #2: Use the Draft or Send Later feature on your e-mail. Proofread and reread every one of your cyber-communications before you send it—because once it's gone, it's out there—*forever*.

RULE #3: Make it easy to read. I recommend using fonts that have serifs—like Times Roman or Garamond—those little extra marks on the ends of some letters. They help the reader to scan the line. Also, avoid using ALL CAPITALS in your e-mails. They are difficult to read and also indicate yelling or projecting anger.

RULE #4: Avoid textspeak and emoticons. Textspeak is the art of abbreviating: CUL8R for "see you later." In texts and 140-character tweets it makes sense to use them, but if the person reading an e-mail or letter from you has to work at deciphering your message, you've failed to communicate. Emoticons should be avoided in formal business e-mails or when writing a person you don't know well.

RULE #5: Use a salutation. Start your e-mail with "Dear Jim," just "Jim," or "Dear Mr. Jacobs." When writing to a group, use the group name such as Marketing Team or Sales Group. Use a formal title when writing to someone you've never met or don't know well.

LETTERS AND MEMOS

Finally, we come to letters and memos: real, physical communications processed on paper or sometimes even handwritten with a pen.

Here's a weird truth in the e-mail age: These days, real letters delivered through the postal service or by an overnight carrier or hand-carried by a personal courier have become the means of communicating when you want to say, "This is really important," or "This is really personal," or when you want to thank someone in the most respectful way possible. Snail mail stands out.

28

EVERYDAY BUSINESS MANNERS

As we saw in Chapter 27, the way you handle yourself matters in business: Exhibiting demeaning behaviors or a superior attitude can and will have a powerfully negative effect on the way your colleagues view you. When it comes to everyday manners, the impact is more subtle—but here, too, the judgments that others make about you can mean the difference between your success or failure.

GENDER-NEUTRAL BUSINESS

Men are not supposed to treat a woman any differently than they would another man. Personally, I've never held a chair for a man—and in fact, proper business etiquette says that a man should *not* hold the chair for a woman. The problem men face here is that many women—at least many of those who responded to our survey—still want a man to hold a chair for them at a work-related social dinner. Suddenly, this black-and-white rule becomes murky gray.

The key to solving any business etiquette dilemma is to apply the principles of etiquette in a thoughtful way: At a casual business lunch, I would follow the standard guideline and refrain from holding the chair for a female colleague. If I'm seated next to a female colleague at an elegant business dinner, as we approach our chairs I will look over at her and ask, "May I get your chair for you?" Now I've made it *her* choice, and she can respond in whatever way makes her feel most comfortable: "No, thank you, I'm all set,"—or "Why, yes, Peter. Thank you."

Rather than simply holding the chair and risking offending my coworker, consideration requires me to ask her what her preference is. By asking this question, I acknowledged the guideline in a way that made both of us feel comfortable—and that is what etiquette is all about.

AROUND THE OFFICE

Mr. or Ms.?

When you start a new job, one of the first issues you'll face as a new employee is how you should address your colleagues. Watch, listen, and learn. Be an observer of human behavior—then emulate what you see others doing. If everyone else calls your boss Ms. Smith, the odds are very good that you should do the same. Don't be shy about asking your coworkers for advice. When in doubt, it's always better to defer to the formal when addressing administrative staff or anyone senior to you, and wait to be invited to use a first name.

ETIQUETTE IMPERATIVE
Workplace Cultures

Every workplace you enter is a new culture with its own rules. Your job is to learn these rules and work within them.

Whatever the situation, if you are unsure of what to do, watch the people around you for clues and follow their lead.

Gossip

Wherever men and women gather for work, tongues will wag. People talk behind other people's backs in every office—so why shouldn't you get in on the act, too?

Here's why: Gossip creates hard feelings. Hard feelings and the other distractions stemming from rude behavior at the workplace lower employee morale. Productivity takes a hit, and employee retention can suffer. Ultimately, all these factors drive down profits, and if profits go south, you're going to feel it in your pocketbook—or worse.

So make a pact with yourself: Don't gossip.

If you see others gossiping, what should you do? At the very least, refuse to participate by leaving the conversation at once. Or you can go one step better, by letting the group know how you feel: "Hey, let's back off. Please." Then change the subject: "Anyway, I'm more interested in whether anyone saw the Yankees blow that three-run lead and lose to the Red Sox. Can you believe they did that?"

Cubicle Etiquette

Cubicles are here to stay. As an effective way for businesses to maximize the value of office space, they're unbeatable. But while a cubicle offers a modicum of privacy, it's not the same as having an office with a door that you can shut. The problems that occur in cubicles usually have to do with this lack of a private space. These include the following:

NOISE. The background hum in an open office is bad enough. When you add loud conversations (either in person or over the phone), you have a recipe for real frustration. *Noise interferes with a person's ability to work.* While you can't do much about the normal background noise in your area, you can work to keep the noise you generate to a minimum by lowering your voice and using headphones when listening to music.

CONVERSATIONS. A short Q & A session with a colleague is fine—but a longer consultation or a group discussion should be taken to a conference room, an available private office, or the break room. If private space is not available, you and your visitor(s) will need to learn to talk quietly.

PHONE VOICE. Make a conscious effort to lower your voice. Men, in particular, tend to talk louder than normal when they get on a phone.

SPEAKERPHONES. See Chapter 27, pages 198–199.

PERSONAL PHONE CALLS. See Chapter 8, pages 48–52.

BURPS, SLURPS, SMACKS. Smacking gum, burping, slurping coffee— these noises travel and are offensive to others. A quick nose blow is okay, but if you have to clear your sinuses and need to go at it with gusto, take it to the restroom.

THE CUBICLE WALL. The neat thing about cubicles is how easy they make it for a person to pop his head above the cubicle wall and interject himself into a conversation in the next cubicle. Don't. Instead, walk around and enter your neighbor's cubicle through the entrance, as you would an office. Otherwise, it looks like you're eavesdropping. I realize it can be hard to intentionally ignore a conversation in the next cubicle— but it's your responsibility to show respect for other people's privacy by not jumping up and showing them that you've been listening in.

The Unisex Restroom

- The office should decide on seat up or down, then leave it that way.

- Keep the door shut and locked when in use.

- Leave it immaculate for the next person.

Gifts

The only appropriate way for employees to give a gift to a manager is as a group. Otherwise, acknowledge the birthday on the day in question by saying, "Happy Birthday." And, if you want, give him a birthday card.

Holiday gift giving is another source of workplace angst. Should you buy a gift for everyone in your office? Answer: no. Offices usually have a tradition of some kind about holiday gifts, such as the Secret Santa or Yankee Swap with gift values held to a small dollar amount.

It's fine to go ahead and give a gift to one or two people you're especially close to, but do the gift giving in private, out of the sight and hearing of other employees. Remember, your goal is to show your appreciation to a specific person.

Finally, just because you give someone a gift, don't expect one in return.

Gum Chewing

I'm surprised by the number of times I get asked, "What do I do with my gum when I arrive at a meeting?" My first thought is, *"What were you doing arriving at a meeting (or a dinner or a lunch) with gum in your mouth?"*

Quiet gum chewing is perfectly acceptable at your desk when you are alone and not talking on the phone as long as your company doesn't have a "no gum" policy. But the moment someone joins you to have a conversation, discreetly lose the gum. The moment your phone rings, get rid of the gum. As you get up to leave your desk to meet a person or attend a meeting or event, wrap and toss the gum in your wastebasket as you leave.

If you make the mistake of actually arriving with gum in your mouth, either excuse yourself to the restroom where you can dispose of it or swallow it.

The Kitchen and Food

We have had three kitchen wars at my advertising agency. Each one was over a different issue, and each one almost resulted in the kitchen being shut down for good.

The first war involved food theft. Someone's leftovers disappeared one day and that person was *not* happy. The guideline here is really simple: What's yours is yours—and what's not yours, you leave alone.

The second war was over the refrigerator. Some food containers had been left in there so long that they'd started taking on a life of their own. Solution: We asked everyone to be vigilant about removing any old lunches or snacks. Everyone's gotten better about this, and we still have a refrigerator.

The third war was over the dirty plates and glasses left in the sink. It boggles my imagination as to how this could even be a problem. Where's the ambiguity here? You use a plate or a glass, you bring it to the sink, you wash it, you dry it, and you put it away.

The Watercooler

A quick work break is a great thing. It's an opportunity to stretch your legs, shake out the cobwebs, and recharge yourself. But there are some problems that can arise, especially if you have a couple of coworkers who are in the habit of taking a break at the same time you do.

BREAKING TOO OFTEN: Taking a break once in the morning and once in the afternoon makes sense. Taking a break every fifteen minutes, however, will quickly mark you as a shirker.

BREAKING TOO LONG: Be careful—a ten-minute break can suddenly grow into a half-hour break. Then, before you know it, tongues are wagging and managers are scowling.

INAPPROPRIATE CONVERSATION: An increasing number of companies now have rules outlining appropriate and inappropriate topics for office conversation. Jokes may be acceptable in one company and taboo in another. Gossiping is never acceptable. The same goes for trash-talking the company and/or its policies. Instead, focus on "safe" subjects such as movies, sports, entertainment, and music. And if the conversation veers where it shouldn't, excuse yourself and head back to work.

HYGIENE

People who don't wash often enough, or who don't use a deodorant and consequently smell unpleasant, are hurting their opportunity to have good relationships with colleagues and negatively impacting their chances for promotion. The easiest way to deal with the problem is to wash regularly—once a day—and use a deodorant, preferably one with little or no scent. Fresh clothes each day are another must. At the very least, give your shirt or other clothes the sniff test—and be honest with yourself about the results.

The other big problem area involves scents—cologne, perfume, or scented deodorants. Splashing on the cologne or perfume might make heads turn when you walk by—but maybe for the wrong reason. In fact, many organizations now have "no-scent" policies.

ETIQUETTE IMPERATIVE
What to Wear

If people focus on your clothes rather than on you, then you've chosen the wrong clothes to wear.

CLOTHING

Clothing is a difficult issue. What you consider to be casually appropriate, your boss may consider to be inappropriate. When you're dressing for work, keep this point in mind: If there's a company dress policy and your clothes breach that policy, then people will focus on your clothes, not on you.

If you wear a pair of jeans and a collarless shirt to the office and everyone else is wearing a coat and tie, your clothes will make you stand out. If you wear a three-piece suit to an interview, on the other hand, and the people interviewing you are all wearing polo shirts and khakis, then they may be distracted by your clothes, and not focus on you.

To help you dress for success, including the tricky distinction between business casual and business professional attire, here are some guidelines:

PROFESSIONAL

ACCEPTABLE

Suits—three-piece, two-piece, two-buttoned or three-buttoned, vest (optional)

Blazers or sports jacket

Slacks

Dress shirts or Oxford-style button-down collars with tie

Dark socks

Oxfords, wingtips, or dress loafers

Overcoats or raincoat

NOT ACCEPTABLE

Loud colors or bold patterns

Wearing a spread collar without a tie

Athletic shoes

White socks

Fur coats

Showy belt buckles

Visible gold chains or flashy jewelry

CASUAL

ACCEPTABLE

Blazers or sports jacket

Shirts—Oxford-style button-down collars, tie optional

Turtleneck shirts

Short-sleeved, collared knit polo shirts

Khaki slacks

V-neck or crewneck sweaters

Informal ties

Dark socks

Loafers or other comfortable shoes

NOT ACCEPTABLE

T-shirts with slogans, sayings, or cartoons

Torn or worn-out jeans

Anything too shiny or too tight

Sandals

Tank tops

Shorts

Does Business Casual Mean
That I Can Wear Jeans and a T-Shirt?

The issue of whether jeans are allowed or not is determined by the policy of each individual workplace. In some places jeans are fine, and in others they are not. It is *never* acceptable, however, to wear jeans that are torn, have holes in them, are stained, are too tight, and/or are very worn out. This applies to both men and women.

The same guidelines apply to T-shirts: In some companies, for example, wearing the company T-shirt with a logo is perfectly acceptable, but that's all. If T-shirts are allowed at your office, your shirts should always be clean, in good condition, and slogan free.

29

BUSINESS SOCIAL EVENTS

It's three o'clock in the afternoon, just another ordinary working day, when suddenly the phone rings. It's your company's sales manager at the other end of the line: "Tom, I just got off the phone with Bill Jones at Aerospace. They signed the contract today. I'm hosting a dinner tomorrow night to celebrate. You worked hard on the details, so I was hoping you might join us."

Your sales manager is right: You *did* work hard, and celebrating the victory with the client will be a real honor. Congratulations!

Now . . . be careful.

The dinner with client and colleagues is a business function, not a social function—even if it is a "celebration." No matter how relaxed the atmosphere is, and no matter how friendly and collegial everybody feels, how you conduct yourself at the dinner will reflect on you the next day and in the future.

This holds true for every business social event you will ever take part in—not to mention many events that don't even appear to be business related.

Business social events offer an opportunity to combine pleasure with work, particularly the relationship-building aspect of work—and that's exactly the part that can either bolster your success or hurt it. Whether you're schmoozing at a business social hour, attending a sit-down dinner, or going on a business-related outing, etiquette can make all the difference as to how well you connect with other people.

THE BUSINESS SOCIAL MIXER

There are several versions of the business social mixer: It could be an internal office cocktail event, or a company-sponsored event for clients and prospects, or an event hosted by a client, or an association event (such as a local chamber of commerce mixer) at which you're representing your company, or an event that's held as part of a conference or seminar.

Whatever the nature of the gathering, the key point to keep in mind is that your company hasn't asked you to attend simply to eat, drink, and have a good time. At all of these events—with the possible exception of the internal company gathering—you will be expected to mix and mingle, to meet new people, and to develop new contacts while also building on your existing relationships.

Introductions

Before you walk in the door at one of these events, you need to know how to introduce yourself and others correctly. Introductions are the first moment of interaction, and they form the basis of people's first impressions. It's imperative that you get the introduction right. When you do, each participant will feel comfortable and ready to move on to getting to know the other person better. When you blow an introduction, the focus shifts to the mistake, and the opportunity to ignite a new relationship is lost.

Check the tips on meeting and greeting in Chapter 10.

Alcohol

At all business social events, the single biggest source of trouble is alcohol. If you are even slightly inebriated, you won't be able to concentrate fully on your real task of fostering new relationships and enhancing existing ones. If you want to have an alcoholic beverage, have just one and nurse it slowly to make it last. Or you can make things even easier on yourself by forgoing alcohol completely. In today's business world, it's perfectly respectable not to imbibe at all. Soda water, soda, juice, or non-alcoholic beer are acceptable alternatives.

Conversing

Many people are petrified at the idea of starting a conversation with a stranger at a business social function. Fortunately, you can get over this fear. Here are three tricks that will really help:

1. Practice, practice, practice. Get into the habit of talking to "safe strangers" whenever you encounter them, including taxicab drivers, salesclerks, checkout counter people, the FedEx delivery person, and so on.

2. Keep up to date on a variety of topics. Sports, politics, entertainment, music, popular books, movies, business news (especially in your field), and travel are all topics that most people have at least some interest in and enjoy talking about.

3. Ask people their opinion. In step 2 you identified some topics. Now frame the topic as a question and ask for the person's opinion. You've just given him the permission to talk. And talk he will while you look like a good conversationalist.

Handing Out Your Business Card

I'm amazed when I see people toss business cards around a table like they're dealing a poker hand. A business card is an extension of the person and should be treated with respect.

- If the person you're giving a card to outranks you, wait until she offers hers to you first.

- With people of equal rank, go ahead, you can offer your card first.

- Use a card case to keep your cards in perfect condition.

- When you receive a card, look at it. And after you look at it, put it away carefully; don't just stuff it in a pocket.

Working the Room

The business social event is a terrific opportunity to land new business, solidify existing relationships, and discover new candidates for future prospecting. The craft of "working the room"—making your way steadily and purposefully from person to person—provides you with a chance to meet and interact with lots of people. Not only is this skill helpful to you in broadening your network, but as you master the art of being a good conversationalist, other people will recognize your talent and be impressed by it.

The following tips will help you work any room effectively:

Before you go to the event . . .

SET GOALS FOR YOURSELF. By that, I *don't* mean how many shrimp you can eat. Develop a list of people you want to meet and a plan of action for meeting them.

RESEARCH. Once you've developed this list, find out more about the people you hope to meet. Learn about their background and their non-business interests—then record this information in your contact management system so you have it at your fingertips for future use.

When you're at the event . . .

STAND UP AND WALK AROUND THE ROOM. Don't sit in one place or stand in one corner the entire time.

MOVE OUT OF YOUR COMFORT ZONE. Challenge yourself: Don't stand there safely talking shop with your coworkers all evening long. Instead, consciously choose to approach people you don't know, introduce yourself, and strike up a conversation. When you are in a conversation, make sure you include all the other people in the group. The more you do this, the easier it will get.

WATCH FOR CLUES AS YOU APPROACH PEOPLE. Observe their body language for signs of receptivity. Listen to how they welcome you (or don't) into their conversation. Not everybody will be receptive to your approach. If someone blows you off, move on to someone else.

OPEN CONVERSATIONS ON AN UPBEAT NOTE. Always start with a positive comment or question. Don't be negative, either in tone or substance. Use open-ended questions to promote dialogue.

LOOK FOR TOPICS OF COMMON INTEREST. If you are at a person's house for a business dinner, look around for clues to their interests in photos, objects, and books.

SEEK OUT NEW AND DIFFERENT PEOPLE. Relish the opportunity to bridge generational and cultural gaps.

CONNECT AND THEN MOVE ON. After a few minutes of conversation, gently excuse yourself from the group you're with and move on to another person or group.

Remember, since you're representing your company, the way you handle yourself will reflect on you and on your employer. Don't be surprised if word gets back to others in your company about how you conducted yourself—be it good or bad.

Breaking Up a Monopoly

Despite your best efforts, every now and then at a business social event you'll find yourself cornered by someone who latches on and won't let go. You know your mission is to mix and mingle—so how do you extricate yourself from a conversation with a monopolizer without being rude or dishonest? Simply be firm and disengage—but do it tactfully: "Jerry, it's been a pleasure catching up with you—but my boss laid it on the line with me today. I need to work the room and make some new contacts tonight. So, if you'll excuse me, I see one of the people I'm supposed to talk with. Maybe we can reconnect later. Take care." And then step away.

THE BUSINESS MEAL

The business meal is a great opportunity to cement a relationship. It's also a great opportunity to ruin one. There are no job skills to fall back on: Everything rests on how you present yourself, how you interact with the other people at the meal, and how you represent your company.

Five Minutes Early Beats Five Minutes Late

I met Jim at a seminar, and he told me the following story: Jim understands the value of being on time and of knowing the culture you are in. His friend doesn't. The friend, a salesman, traveled to the Netherlands to do a deal. His European hosts invited him to a luncheon, and he showed up late. Shortly after that, the European hosts informed Jim that his friend would not get the deal. How could they expect him to make good on his promises, they explained to Jim, if he couldn't even show up on time at a restaurant?

If you are hosting the business meal, be sure to be there five to ten minutes early. This will give you a chance to check the table and make sure everything is acceptable, and to figure out where people will sit. If you plan to serve wine, talk with the maître d' or wine steward about an appropriate selection. One especially nice touch is to arrange for payment of the bill ahead of time, so you don't have to deal with a check arriving at the table at the end of the meal. Finally, hit the men's room, do what you need to, then wash your hands, comb your hair, and make sure you are looking sharp.

If you are unavoidably delayed for some reason, call the restaurant (of course you were smart enough to write down the phone number before leaving your office, right?), ask them to let your host know that you're running late, and give an estimate of when you think you'll arrive.

ETIQUETTE IMPERATIVE
Who Pays?

It's simple, really. At a business meal, whoever does the inviting pays.

When You're the Host

If you are the host of a business meal, you should:

- Arrange for the reservation.

- Do the inviting.

- Make sure your cell phone and pager are turned off.

- Make or facilitate introductions.

- Indicate where you would like people to sit, making especially sure to offer the best seat to the most important guest (usually by seating that person to your right).

- Help people with the menu selections by suggesting a couple of particularly good items (of course you've been careful to choose a restaurant that you've been to before, so you know what is especially good).

- Select wine for the table.

- Direct the conversation by introducing topics.

- Watch to make sure that all the guests are engaged and enjoying themselves, and that no one is stuck being a wallflower.

- Introduce any business discussion *after* the main course has been completed.

- Pay the bill.

- Finally, at the end of the meal, indicate when it's time to depart, and thank everyone for coming.

When You're the Guest

If you are the guest at a business meal, you should:

- Watch for clues from your host as to where he or she wants you to sit.

- Make sure your cell phone and pager are turned off.

- Listen to and take part in the conversation, but don't dominate it.

- Introduce yourself to and converse with the people seated on both your right and your left.

- Order a moderate, midpriced meal—unless the host insists that you try the "best filet mignon in the state."

- Order a drink only if your host and others order drinks as well—and then nurse that drink along slowly. If others at the table do choose to order drinks or wine, there is no imperative saying that you have to join in—fruit juice, sparkling water, or soda are all excellent alternatives.

- Conduct yourself with the best table manners possible (see Chapter 20)—and when you are not sure what to do, watch to see what others are doing, then imitate them. If that doesn't work, then make a choice based on doing whatever you think shows the most consideration for the people around you.

- Wait for your host to bring up any business topics. Typically, at a business dinner, business talk is engaged in only after the main course is completed. At a business breakfast or lunch, you can begin talking business after the orders have been placed. Since the host invited you, it's up to him or her to bring up any business issues.

- At the end of the meal, thank your dining partners and your host. Then, when you get home, or the first thing next morning at the office, handwrite a thank-you note.

AFTERWORD

Throughout this book, I've mentioned again and again that situations arise for which there is no specific manners rule. That's when I use the essential principles of etiquette—consideration, respect, and honesty—to figure out what to do.

START WITH CONSIDERATION. Be aware of how a current situation *affects* everyone involved.

SHOW RESPECT FOR EACH PERSON INVOLVED. Think of several possible courses of action and examine how each solution affects each person.

BE HONEST WITH YOURSELF. Be truthful with yourself as you select the solution that best solves the problem for *all* the people involved.

Each time you use the three principles to help identify the best course of action, the outcome for you is the same: confidence. When you feel confident, you exude confidence. When you exude confidence, people trust you and react positively to you. People like to associate with people they trust.

That is why etiquette is valuable to you. Use it, enjoy how people respond to you, and watch yourself become ever more successful in your daily life, your social life, and your work life. Good luck!

ACKNOWLEDGMENTS

I want to offer a very special thank-you to Royce Flippin, who worked tirelessly with me to edit my rambling, run-on writing into a readable text.

Cindy Post Senning and Elizabeth Upham Howell were invaluable as they read every chapter and made sure I stayed on topic. With her expert's knowledge about etiquette, Peggy Post kept my advice on point.

Thank you to Jessica McGrady, Toni Sciarra, and Greg Chaput for their understanding, patience, and insightful editing.

Many thanks go to Katherine Cowles, my agent, who believed in this project right from the start and encouraged me to pursue it when I wasn't sure it would ever fly.

Anna Post and Lizzie Post are wonderful daughters who have drawn on their own experiences to help me fine-tune the etiquette advice.

Finally, I want to thank my great-grandmother Emily Post. I have spent a great deal of time reading her original *Etiquette* as well as her novels and other nonfiction books. The more I read and learn about her, the more I realize what a truly extraordinary woman she was. Long before she wrote *Etiquette*, she understood what it meant to be gracious and courteous—or, as she called it, "to have charm." If ever there was a person who had charm, it was she.

INDEX

EMILY POST, 1872 TO 1960

Emily Post began her career as a writer at the age of thirty-one. Her romantic stories of European and American society were serialized in *Vanity Fair, Collier's, McCall's,* and other popular magazines. Many were also successfully published in book form.

Upon its publication in 1922, her book, *Etiquette,* topped the nonfiction bestseller list, and the phrase "according to Emily Post" soon entered our language as the last word on the subject of social conduct. Mrs. Post, who as a girl had been told that well-bred women should not work, was suddenly a pioneering American career woman. Her numerous books, a syndicated newspaper column, and a regular network radio program made Emily Post a figure of national stature and importance throughout the rest of her life.

"Good manners reflect something from inside—an innate sense of consideration for others and respect for self."

—Emily Post

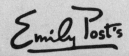

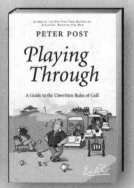

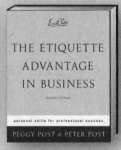